Meditating with Character

Meditating
with Character

Kamalamani

BOOKS

Winchester, UK
Washington, USA

First published by O-Books, 2012
O-Books is an imprint of John Hunt Publishing Ltd., Laurel House, Station Approach,
Alresford, Hants, SO24 9JH, UK
office1@o-books.net
www.o-books.com

For distributor details and how to order please visit the 'Ordering' section on our website.

Sangharakshita (1995) *Complete Poems 1941/1994*. Windhorse Publications

Design: Stuart Davies

Printed in the UK by CPI Antony Rowe
Printed in the USA by Edwards Brothers Malloy

We operate a distinctive and ethical publishing philosophy in all
areas of our business, from our global network of authors to
production and worldwide distribution.

CONTENTS

For Ladybird, Pali and the ancestors

Foreword

What most fascinates me about character is its constantly paradoxical nature. Character is our way of both evading and engaging with the world; it is how we express ourselves, and how we protect ourselves from being seen. Our character structure offers us a key to the meaning of life – and also encourages us to try the same old key on every door we encounter. It both wards off embodiment, and enables us to be embodied beings.

It should be evident from this that character is a modern way of talking about some of the things that enlightenment traditions have been describing for generations. Character theory points out that what causes us suffering is not so much what we feel, but how we feel about it; not so much what we do, but how we do it. As Kamalamani paraphrases her teacher Sangharakshita, "There is nothing wrong with our experience; it is our *interpretation* of our experience which is the problem."

Thus I have often noticed that people in therapy get stuck in an attempt to *change without changing* – that is, they use exactly the same style in trying to live differently that they have always used to live in the way they are unhappy with. This doesn't work very well, because most of our problems can actually be traced back to the style in which we do things. For example, someone comes to therapy suffering from addictions; they leap on the therapy and grab hold of it, immediately feeling that it is the only thing keeping them going and they can't live without it. Or someone else comes because they feel that life is meaningless; at once they start criticising the therapist and picking apart everything they are offered. We all attempt to 'do therapy' in exactly the way we are accustomed to doing everything else.

Therapists, like spiritual teachers, are therefore constantly aware of huge amounts of wasted effort being expended, as

1

people energetically dig themselves further into their favourite hole. How to stop digging? How to relax and let things, including ourselves, be as they are? These are the sorts of questions that therapy and spiritual practice share. For me, one of the attractive things about Buddhism is that it invites us to study our experience, without (in theory at least) defining in advance what the result of that study will be; this is very similar to what I try to do as a therapist. At the same time, of course, therapy like Buddhism has acquired some ideas as what we are likely to find out by studying our experience; and I find character theory one of the most important of these.

Character theory has only become fully helpful through shedding its *pathologising* aspect. Like many features of psychotherapy, character historically has a medical, diagnostic function, as a way of deciding what is wrong with people. Realising that it is not a malfunction, but basically just *a way of being a person*, which can work creatively, destructively or somewhere in between depending on the circumstances of life, has enabled us to see that the character structure which traps people into unhelpful styles of being *is itself the way out of the trap*. It is not by becoming someone different that we free ourselves, but by becoming more fully who we are.

As Kamalamani so clearly describes, meditation is a brilliant way to engage with this process. Just as with other aspects of life, we meditate *in character*: it brings us directly into contact with our own deepest habits of being, our individual style of aversion, craving and delusion. If we can contemplate our style of being in clarity, without heaping on to it further layers of aversion, craving and delusion, then our life may become radically simplified. This is what meditation in the Buddhist tradition has always been about; by bringing it together with character theory, Kamalamani offers a new and helpful way of conceiving the process, together with a number of practical tools.

It is every teacher's dream to have their own knowledge

reflected back to them having passed through an autonomous subjectivity and taken on independent form. This warm, witty, wise and incisive book fulfils that dream for me: while I recognise many of the ideas here, I could not have expressed them in this way myself, or applied them to the material Kamalamani uses. I have learnt a good deal from it, and I hope and expect that you will do the same. I very much like the concept of the 'spiritual friend' which appears in several traditions; and it came up for me strongly in reading *Meditating with Character* – this is a truly *friendly* book!

Nick Totton

Preface

Meditating with Character was born from a waking dream. I awoke on the last morning of the final session of my Diploma in 'Embodied-Relational Therapy' training with a strong sense to write about 'character positions' in relationship to the practice of meditation. Character positions are a body of knowledge from psychotherapy which were a foundation of my training and are a backbone of this book. That was more than two years ago. Weaving a dreaming thought into my first published book has been a path with many interesting twists and turns. In my late father's word, it has been "character-building" (no pun intended).

This book is an experiment and an invitation. The experiment aspect is that it brings together areas from meditation and Body psychotherapy in a largely process-oriented way. This material is presented in the nature of an invitation. Those of you who are intermediate meditators are invited to go deeper in your awareness of your embodiment in the context of your meditation practice. It is also an invitation for the more seasoned meditators, body workers and 'spiritual' practitioners amongst you who have an experiential interest in the nature of bodymind. (I tend to use the term 'bodymind' throughout this book to remind myself of the significance of experiencing mind as integral to the body and body as integral to the mind.)

Being an experiment, I have no idea how this book will be received. My motivation for writing it is that I have experienced first hand the usefulness of reflecting upon character positions (as well as through training with therapy colleagues, in working with therapy clients and drawing upon a lifetime of people-watching). Character positions can help to make sense of life conditioning and how that has shaped our experience of being a body, living on the body of the planet. I am personally looking

5

forward to using this book myself as a resource in the months to come as I spend more time on my meditation cushion and slightly less time writing. I hope you find it useful in exploring your meditation practice.

May all blessings be yours.

Kamalamani

Bristol, January 2011

Acknowledgements

Writing a book can feel like an incredibly solitary activity. Yet the truth is that there are many people who have been supportive mid-wives (and mid-husbands) in this book's arrival. I wish to thank those who have taught me so much as a practising Buddhist, a counsellor and as an Embodied-Relational Therapist.

In bringing each of you to mind I am reminded of the image of Indra's net. Indra was an Indian king (in Hindu mythology), with a net stretching as far as the eye could see – through infinite time and space. At each point of intersection between the myriad threads of the web was a jewel. Each jewel reflected every other jewel in this vast net of interconnections, with the beauty of one jewel being reflected in all the others. This image reminds me of how we are brought together in this web of interconnections through life, and the appreciation I feel for so many people.

With Indra's net in mind, I thank the teachers who have taught me about Buddhism. Thanks to Achalavajra (now known as Bill Hard), my earliest meditation and Dharma teacher (Dharma refers to the Buddha's teachings). I thank my dear friend and private preceptor, Maitreyi, who gave me the name, 'Kamalamani', at the point of ordination into the Triratna Buddhist Order.

I am greatly appreciative of Urgyen Sangharakshita, the founder of the Order. Without his creativity, insight and lifelong work as a translator of the Dharma, I doubt I would be practising Buddhism today. There are numerous other teachers from the Triratna Buddhist Order and the wider Buddhist world to whom I feel indebted for their work and writing, including but by no means limited to Vessantara, Aya Khema, Jack Kornfield and Joanna Macy.

I appreciate my clients and the work I have done with them, particularly in reflecting upon character positions in my therapy practice. I am struck again and again by the amazing courage and tenacity of the human heart. I am very grateful to my counselling and therapy teachers and supervisors whose teaching and experience has given me the basis of knowledge, understanding and practical experience to have written this book. I am also very thankful to the various therapists and body workers with whom I have worked as a client.

I am particularly grateful to Nick Totton and Allison Priestman with whom I trained in 'Embodied-Relational Therapy', a particular form of Body psychotherapy. Thanks to Allison for her gentle holding and presence. Thanks to Nick for his immense skill, expertise, and ethical sensitivity. I have learned more about myself and my clients in training with Nick – witnessing his work and working with him as a supervisee – than from anyone else. I am also appreciative of Em Edmondson, who originally worked with Nick in developing the character positions as they are presented here. Nick's presentation of character positions during my training was central in preparing this book.

Thanks to interested friends. I am most grateful to Sarah Thorne. Sarah's support and shared enthusiasm for the themes presented here have been very precious indeed. She has shown an uncanny knack of contacting me on the days when I have nearly given up writing this book. Thanks to Sarah, Sally Rawlings, Nick Totton, and my partner, Suhada, for reading very early drafts of this book.

Thanks also to Paramananda, Nick Totton, and Chris Wilson for their useful comments on the first draft of my book. Thanks to Vidyamala for her early support as I began to look for a publisher. Thanks to Caroline Brazier for her very helpful words of encouragement, particularly during the latter stages of writing and editing. Thanks to those friends and colleagues I have interviewed about their meditation practice, in particular: Daman, Pamela Crummay, Penny Kennington, Isla Macdonald, Sally

Rawlings, Sarah Thorne, Shraddhalocani, and Suhada, and so many others who have shared their meditation experiences over the years. Thanks also to my Mum, Pamela Crummay, for encouraging me to wear purple since the age of four.

Finally, heartfelt thanks to Suhada. Suhada's name, translated from the Pali, means 'good-hearted friend' and he has certainly embodied his name in his patient, kind, loving, loyal steadfastness.

Introduction

Again and yet again work on whatever estranges you from meditation!
Lay bare whatsoever arises, good and bad thoughts alike!
The child who knows his way, carries along on the path
every harmless thing he happens upon and nothing that harms him.
Tsogyal, 2008: 689

Meditating with Character stands at a confluence. This confluence is the meeting point between Buddhist meditation and Body psychotherapy. Meditation seems to be in vogue. When I first learnt to meditate sixteen years ago, meditation was still seen as something of an alternative, 'fringe' activity. It is now much more accepted in mainstream culture, to the extent that mindfulness-based meditation approaches are used for stress reduction, living with pain (Burch, 2008 and Kabat-Zinn, 2005) and for working with depression (Williams, Teasdale, Segal and Kabat-Zinn, 2007). There has lately been a renewed sense of interest amongst Buddhist meditators in connecting more fully with the body in meditation (see for example Ray, 2008 and Johnson, 2000). And in the past decade there has been a rising tide of interest in Body psychotherapy in therapeutic circles (Totton 2003: 1). In writing this book it has been fascinating to work at a confluence which is the focal point of such energy, synchronicity and interest.

The wider landscape surrounding the confluence of this particular book has been shaped by my interest in the fields of sustainable development and ecopsychology. These fields are relevant to meditation, Buddhism and Body psychotherapy because they are concerned with interconnection. In exploring interconnection inwardly (tapping into our connection with our bodymind in meditation) we enter the realm of embodiment. By embodiment, I mean the sense we make of being present with a bodymind (both on and off our meditation cushions). Understanding our own embodiment is inextricably linked to the sense we make of living on the much larger body of the planet – as one amongst billions of human beings and other than human beings.

As we become more aware of both our embodiment and our process in meditation the more equipped we become to understand – and experience – our interconnectedness with all other life: human and other than human. In reading *Meditating with Character* you are invited into an awareness of all sentient life and living processes – local and global – through engaging fully with your own precious life and your meditation practice. You are invited to review your meditation practice and conditioning to date, through drawing upon the body of knowledge from Body psychotherapy known as character positions. The six character positions (named: boundary, oral, control, holding, thrusting, and crisis) are a particular way of looking at our processes of embodiment and disembodiment.

Each of the character positions relate specifically to the developmental stages of baby and childhood which are common to all human beings. These are: being conceived and being born, learning to feed and be nurtured, testing independence, learning rules and routines, experimenting with wilfulness, and taking on a gendered identity in the world. Exploring the character positions throws light on our approaches to being a body and the stories of our lives. These are reflected in the styles and strategies we have adopted since our conception (and through past lives).

For example, we may notice that our personal strategies focus specifically upon meeting our needs, in which case we may resonate with the oral character position. Or if we consistently and determinedly assert our will we may find we are patterned by the thrusting character position. Character positions can illuminate how our embodiment is expressed and reflected in our prevailing life themes, our body shape, habits, resistances and patterning. An experiential knowledge of character positions can be invaluable in helping us to understand our patterns and habits as a meditator.

As well as being concerned with strategies, character explores physical 'armouring' that developed in our body in response to situations which we perceived to be threatening and dangerous. This armouring takes different forms. I am reminded of Jack Kornfield's description of armouring; the first I came across as a new meditator:

... most often the kinds of pains we encounter in meditative attention are not indications of physical problems. They are the painful, physical manifestations of our emotional, psychological, and spiritual holding and contractions. Reich called these pains our muscular armor, the areas of our body that we have tightened over and over in painful situations as a way to protect ourselves from life's inevitable difficulties.
Kornfield, 1994: 43

The muscular armouring experienced as pain, tension and energy blocks can be particularly noticeable as we sit in meditation. Having an awareness of muscular armouring is helpful as we learn more about ourselves through our posture and our sense of embodiment in meditation. Psychic armouring manifests in the patterning of our emotional responses and strategies to those early perceived threats. This aspect of armouring fuels our defensive thoughts, feelings and sensations. It is also likely that we arrived in this life with armouring from previous lives, which may make particular sense to those of you who are receptive to the phenomenon of rebirth.

Attending to and being aware of our personal armouring as we explore character can support us in setting up the conditions to loosen these patterns, channelling that energy in more creative ways. As we meditate we can also build upon the existing resourceful and creative aspects of character positioning and our ease and well-being in being a body. It is freeing to understand how we developed different character positions, highlighting what may be very familiar patterns in a more visceral way. Letting go into a greater awareness of our embodied limitations and struggles can free 'held' energies, so that we engage more fully with meditation and the richness of life.

This book is aimed at those of you with some experience of meditation wishing to go deeper in your practice, with a greater awareness of your embodiment. The content is likely to make more sense if your interest is in complementing a 'spiritual' path or journey, particularly a Buddhist path. My aim is that the Buddhist ideas introduced in this book are sufficiently self-explanatory, whether or not you practise Buddhism. This book may also be useful for those of you who are experienced meditators wishing to pay more attention to your embodiment in the context of your practice. This book might also be of interest in exploring your embodied experience – your physical body through to your subtle and astral body – whether or not you meditate regularly.

Going deeper in meditation – if, in reality, there is anywhere to 'go' – can be encouraged by getting to know more intimately your body and its processes in and out of meditation: its workings, secret life, night life, mumblings and moans, ecstatic moments, and what it does and does not like to eat and drink. This can also be encouraged by getting curious about the bits that are less known to you: invisible, bland, numb patches of your skin and body. You may have had urges to ignore, conquer, enjoy, abuse, push, be amazed by, be pained by, be sexy with, be ashamed of, and be rid of, your body – all very human responses. You can go deeper in your embodied meditation through allowing your bodymind to reveal itself more fully to you, through paying it more kindly attention.

Practising meditation and being more aware of your embodiment are by no means 'quick fix' type solutions so sought after in the current cultural climate. As you delve into a greater understanding of your meditation practice and your embodiment you might call upon your sense of curiosity, patience and, perhaps, the loosening of expectations. Understanding character positions is about making sense of who we are and how we got here, in terms of how we adapted in order to live our life and be a bodymind in relationship with those around us and the context into which we were born and raised. It is not about fixing, 'pigeon-holing', making wrong, or pathologising.

This book will explore the following themes:

- Your particular style and approach in relating to yourself and others in meditation.
- Your relationship with your meditation practice now and over time.
- Your process during meditation sessions.
- The notion of embodiment – what this means to you and how and why it matters.
- Your understanding of the body-mind relationship.
- Your resonance with the six character positions.
- Your energetic levels – where energy feels free-flowing and where it feels more stuck or elusive – and how this relates to character positions.
- Listening and attending kindly on an energetic level, becoming aware of your embodied felt senses, perhaps as a new language.
- How your embodiment is influenced by past and present factors, from your ancestral lineage (including family conditioning), karmic lineage, through to your present context.

Engaging with your process
The approach of this book is in the nature of an invitation. It is

also process-oriented, in that it invites you to attend to the process of your own unfurling awareness, rather than advocating a particular set of techniques. We each have a unique relationship with our body: past, present and subject to change in the future, as we grow, get ill, get better, change, age, and approach death.

As you read this book give yourself the time and psychic space to notice your responses and stay with your process. Many of the chapters end with a set of reflections. In using these be receptive to what arrives and *how* it arrives: through images, words, dreams (waking and sleeping), emotion, stories, memories, metaphors, a sense, discomfort, pain, resistance. Stay with this process as fully as you can. Take all the time you need to do this. You might also find it useful to engage in other forms of body work, or techniques such as 'focusing' (Gendlin, 2003) as a means of becoming more adept at tuning into your felt senses.

Set up the conditions to cultivate an awareness of your embodiment in other aspects of your life, rather than just during meditation sessions. As you start to maintain this awareness for more and more prolonged periods (including how, when, and why you become less embodied) you start to sense how the whole of your life can be a practice of compassionate mindfulness and embodied wisdom, rather than simply the formal time you allot to meditation.

Becoming more aware of your embodiment is rather akin to beginning, developing, nurturing and revitalising your meditation practice. It takes time, patience, care and the support of others. In fact, attending to your process of embodiment can be a particular form of meditation, inasmuch as it is concerned with watching and being with your habits, enthusiasm, strategies and blind spots. This book is a creative road map, signposting possible ways towards experiencing a fuller sense of being a bodymind.

There are many different ways you might read and make use of this book. It can be useful to keep a journal. Recording your experiences in a journal can build confidence in keeping track of your different meditation practices. You can look back at your experiences and notice emerging patterns which reflect your inspirations and resistances. The same process can be true in keeping a journal about your embodying experience. Surprising and uncanny things can happen when you relax into a greater sense of receptivity and relate more fully to your experience of being a body. 'Journal' sounds like it simply refers to the written word. You might include other media which capture something about your embodying process.

In engaging with the meditation and reflection exercises you might wish to work with a friend in reading through and following these. You could also experiment with recording yourself reading each of the exercises, using this as an aid in meditation and reflection. This can be useful in encouraging a kindly tone towards yourself which can be a reparative exercise, particularly if you know that you tend towards self-criticism or impatience.

The structure of the book

This book is divided into eight chapters. The first four chapters are about arriving, gathering and scanning the broad landscape – the backdrop for the rest of the book. Chapter 1 reminds you to start from where you are, in your meditation practice and life. Chapter 2 looks at meditation as process. In this chapter you are encouraged to reconnect with your purpose for meditating and to review the journey of your meditation practice thus far. Chapter 3 starts to explore the theme of embodiment and making sense of this by drawing on Buddhist teachings. Chapter 4 sets in context the importance of the theme of embodiment in 21st century life. In looking at the themes of connection, healing and reclaiming, it explores the relevance and significance of cultivating a good enough relationship with our bodies.

The next three chapters introduce character positions.

Chapter 5 explores the relevance of character positions and provides some pointers as to how you might approach this body of knowledge. Chapter 6 introduces the six character positions in detail. In Chapter 7 you are encouraged to start to make sense of character positions in terms of your own life conditioning, with an in-depth series of reflections from the past to the present-day.

Chapter 8 brings together the book's various strands, applying character positions specifically to meditation practice. Each character position is explored again, this time from the point of view of how character positions throw light upon our habits, strengths and weaknesses in our meditation practices. In this chapter each character position is explored in terms of our rationale for turning towards meditation, the potential benefits of meditation for the life strategies of our particular character(s), and the challenges and working edges we may encounter, influenced by particular character positions. Each exploration of the different character positions concludes with reflection and meditation exercises. *Meditating with Character* concludes with some thoughts about further exploration of character positions and meditation.

A word about my use of the words: 'spiritual' and 'spirituality'. I am aware that throughout this book I make reference to these terms. I have misgivings in using them, in that they can mean so many different things to different people. Yet they also have their use. The danger with 'spiritual' and 'spirituality', in my mind, is that they can become a shorthand in somehow assuming we all know what we all mean. This can: (1) be misleading; (2) not reflect the reality of the situation and; (3) gloss over the process of sharing learning and deepening faith through understanding both convergence *and* difference in views about what is 'spiritual'.

I have a sense of what I mean by 'spiritual' and 'spirituality', and urge you to keep a live sense of what they mean (or don't mean) to you in the context of your life and practice. I have kept these words in inverted commas as a reminder to engage with a sense of what you are personally bringing to these words.

Like the teachings of the Buddha, the ideas in this book are another set of fingers pointing at the moon. Like the Buddha's invitation to explore the way of living which he discovered, we have to try and see for ourselves. In the words of Tsongkapa, the fourteenth century founder of the Gelugpa School of Tibetan Buddhism:

> The human body at peace with itself
> Is more precious than the rarest gem.
> Cherish your body, it is yours this one time only.
> The human form is won with difficulty,
> It is easy to lose.
> All worldly things are brief,
> Like lightning in the sky;
> This life you must know
> As the tiny splash of a raindrop;
> A thing of beauty that disappears
> Even as it comes into being.
> Therefore set your goal
> Make use of every day and night
> To achieve it.
> Tsongkapa

Chapter 1

Starting from where you are

The most memorable advice I have been given in learning to meditate was from Achalavarja, one of my first meditation teachers. "Start from where you are," he would say, "there's nowhere else to start!" It was great advice which I still follow – when I remember. Perhaps that's the best advice anyone can give you in learning to meditate (and live): start from where you are and remember to remember. Start from where you are now, this moment. Take a moment, close your eyes, breathe in and breathe out. Notice the rising and falling motion as your breath moves your body. Follow the rhythm of your breath, however and wherever you notice it. Stay with this awareness of your breath for as long as you wish. Starting from where you are is about making the space to connect and seeing what you find (inner-outer, head-toe, earth-sky, self-other).

My starting point this morning: there's a beautiful sunrise out of the window. It's a pink-grey colour. The sky has a wishy-washy texture. The clouds crossing through the yellow-pink sunrays have blurry edges. They are moving swiftly. I wonder how many billions of sunrises the earth has witnessed, yet how each one is unique. I notice I am more in awe of today's sunrise because the sky is clear after a week of snow, ice and slush. I am always slightly amazed that the sun *keeps on rising*. My body feels relaxed and my creativity's flowing. I feel glad to be sitting here, writing and enjoying the elements in the early morning light. I start to type and notice how I feel connected and engaged. I am also struck by how often I feel disconnected and the pain of that disconnection.

Witnessing my life and paying kindly attention to what is

going on in meditation is akin to taking in this sunrise. It can often be the case that our inner witness is trampled by our inner judge, critic, manager and goal-setter. We never quite know what we are going to get from moment to moment in life or meditation. Yet it can be tempting to think we know. That persistent, human game of trying to capture the moment before it's actually happened. It can be easy to fall into the trap of thinking you know what will happen in meditation, what to expect, and how you will work with whatever arises, in terms of the traditional Buddhist 'hindrances' – the things that obscure your focus upon the object of your meditation (see Kamalashila, 1992: 51).

This is the process and dance that happens so often in meditation (and life). Sometimes it seems easier to get caught up in the managed, controlled approach to meditation, in a world where life is so managed and controlled. You might end up doing a rather mechanical version of counting your breath in the mindfulness of breathing (or perhaps it becomes 'the mindfulness of *counting*'). You might feel concentrated and clear thinking from the shoulders upwards, with little warmth or softness below that area of your body. At other times you feel more open and receptive as you start to meditate. You feel well and in good spirits. Perhaps you begin by enjoying your posture, feeling the different sensations in your body, and noticing your environment. The sound of car wheels swishing over the newly fallen rain on the street can sound as pleasant as the birdsong. Your bodymind engages with the practice. Your attention eventually starts to wander down the track of a particular thought, feeling or fantasy. At some point you notice, and kindly and firmly bring your awareness back to the purpose of your meditation.

Perhaps you are at home, on the bus, or standing by a bookshop shelf as you read this. Something urged you to open this book and have a look. Perhaps you're a meditator, perhaps there is nothing shinier to read and you liked the front cover.

How do you feel as you read this chapter? Interested? Bored? (I won't be offended). Keen to read more? Flicking forward to the reflections? Take time to notice *all* of these responses. Notice the words, images, feelings, and thoughts that arise. Notice *how* and *where* these things attract your attention, flirting with your awareness.

The title of this chapter is a misnomer. You can only ever start from where you are. Yet you might sometimes try to start from a more intellectual idea of where you would like to be, or where you were yesterday evening. Perhaps you chase the idea of your moment of perfect happiness, overriding the possibility of this moment revealing itself to you. Approaching and sitting in meditation reflects the microcosm of this dance or tussle between the present embodying moment and an idea of how things should, could or might be; the human mind striving constantly for a new and different experience, pushing, pulling, accepting and rejecting.

The spirit here is to start from where you are now. I invite you to follow this spirit in the process of reading this book. Repeatedly do this, starting over and over, akin to bringing your focus back to the object of your meditation. Through the course of the book you are invited into a fuller and fuller relationship with your embodying, so your reading becomes more like a shared meditation, rather than the imparting of thoughts. This spirit is in keeping with Buddhist teachings, as well as providing a useful basis for looking at character positions, which are the backbone of this book.

Reflections – starting from where you are

Before engaging with the reflections, notice your response to what you have read. Take as much time and space as you can.

Begin by reviewing your current relationship with meditation. What's your immediate starting point, in terms of your practice of and process around meditation?

Reflect upon the current nature of your meditation practice in a practical way e.g. the time of day when you meditate, whether you have a daily practice, the length of your meditations, the form you practice, where you meditate, and whether and how you reflect on your meditation practice when you are not on your cushion.

Contact your current purpose in meditating. Notice what arises without analysing this too much.

Think about particular themes that have emerged in your meditation practice of late, or particular hindrances or obstacles with which you work.

In thinking about your relationship with meditation, whether you have been meditating for ten months or ten years:

1 What have you found straightforward?
2 What have you found challenging?
3 What is your physical experience in meditation?
4 Which meditation practices do you do regularly?
5 What is your relationship with each of these?
6 What distracts you in meditation?
7 What helps you to engage more fully with meditation? E.g. other practices (such as the practise of ethics), particular conditions, support of others etc.
8 What else or who else supports your meditation practice?
9 How has your purpose and reason for meditating changed over time?

In reflecting, notice: thoughts, feeling, emotions, images and memories which arise. Pay as much attention to the process of reflection as the content itself, as you notice your experience.

Chapter 2

Meditation as process

I have often wondered why so many teachers seem to look down on everyday emotions and so-called 'mind stuff', the bulk of mental life... blocking certain sense perceptions in favour of others only hoodwinks the conscious mind. Sensory signals cannot be destroyed by focusing on something else; they are merely repressed. If they are not dealt with directly, they often sidetrack the meditation and make it necessary to spend months or years reaching a state which could have taken minutes if the disturbing thoughts such as greed and jealousy had been processed consciously.
Mindell, 1990: 8

Meditation is a process. Whilst each meditation session has a beginning, various stages and an end, your longer-term relationship with meditation is more open-ended. This relationship, like any relationship, takes various twists and turns over time, like an undulating river in its journey towards the sea. In some phases you may experience very concentrated meditative states, at others you may feel blown and buffeted by the eight traditional Buddhist 'worldly winds' or 'worldly conditions' of: pleasure and pain, loss and gain, fame and infamy, and praise and blame (see Sangharakshita 1998: 7-8). Sometimes you may feel that nothing much is happening (and frankly, you are a bit *bored*). You might have spells when you give up on meditation altogether. It is inevitable (and human) to go through these different phases.

Meditation habits and self-view
You are also likely to have developed views about yourself in

relationship to meditation. Perhaps you hear friends say, "I'm not a meditator," (even though they make effort on the cushion) or, "She's a *really serious* meditator." The chances are that you have your own views, and your own versions of these, about yourself and others. In learning about your meditation practice it is useful to get curious about these views, as well as the habits you have developed in your relationship to meditation over time. Some of these are likely to be really useful, for example, knowing the times of day when it is most effective for you to practise meditation. Other habits might not be quite so useful. It might not be immediately clear to you that you have habits (and rituals) around meditation until you actively reflect on them.

As you become more experienced as a meditator, it can be tempting to think that you are familiar with all of your 'pet' hindrances. It is easy to think that you have it 'sorted'; you have a good understanding of what happens and you know how to work in meditation. It is useful to get an initial sense of your patterns, approaches, hindrances, and habits in this way. In becoming more insightful, and more practiced, it is also vital to stay receptive to how things change (and how that is a central teaching of Buddhism).

Learning meditation is like learning any other new skill – or entering into a new relationship. In the early days there is the importance of learning the technique and listening carefully to the instruction. (Or, in the context of a relationship, gathering information about your friend, lover or workmate.) After that initial phase, you notice your own patterns forming in response to that person or object of focus. The danger at this point and at successive points, is that your stories and views about this object or person become hardened, crystallised and defining. This can be counterproductive given that meditation can be most useful in supporting your understanding of the changing nature of all things, rather than crystallising your stories about yourself and your life. What can be useful in gently dissolving these views (e.g. "I'm not a natural meditator") is to come back again and again to your embodied purpose and intention.

Connecting with your purpose in meditation

Recollecting your purpose can bring a fresh, live sense in taking the initiative, taking stock and taking responsibility. The explicit naming of your purpose can be illuminating, reminding you to start from where you are. For example, when I sit to meditate, bringing my purpose to mind, I may have a 'disturbing thought' (in Mindell's words from the quote above). In my case, this might be: "Not meditation again (sigh), I can't be bothered, I want to go out."

This is really clear information about my starting point. It might not be what I *want* or expect to hear, but at least it's clear and concise! In recalling my purpose, I contact my initial resistance and can choose how to respond to that resistance, getting into fuller dialogue with myself. If I sit to meditate without recollecting my purpose, I am more likely to distract myself and stay out of touch with a live sense of how I am and why I am sitting. Wading through treacle, going foggy-headed and having lead-like legs come to mind.

Inviting your purpose and seeing how this manifests itself is energising and refreshing. When you go for a walk, you put on your waterproofs when it is raining. Connecting with your purpose is the equivalent of checking your internal weather as you sit to meditate. Getting in touch with your purpose might also feel risky, in as much as it might throw light on the fact that you have no idea why you are meditating and where on earth you are. That is gold dust as information about your starting point. Not knowing where you are is neither bad nor wrong – it's just not knowing where you are.

Perhaps being honestly and congruently lost, and at ease with being lost, is something we have yet to learn, particularly if we are Western practitioners of Buddhism. Culturally, we are not well known in the current climate for being at ease with being lost in the wilderness. (Instead we seem to have made a rather good job of degrading our wilderness: internal and external.) Being lost is as good a starting point as any, in terms of providing you with a live thread with your meditation practice.

Entice yourself to get really fascinated about why you meditate, even if you have been meditating for decades. Recalling your purpose at the start of each sit gives you the precious, jewel-like opportunity of a daily return to beginner's mind and a way of clarifying how you see both meditation and yourself. I am reminded of the Buddha of primordial purity, Vajrasattva, encouraging us to see things as fresh, new and as if for the first time (even if we have actually seen that particular thing, person or phenomenon thousands of times before).

It can also be useful to revisit periodically your broader rationale for meditating: your underlying assumptions about meditation. In thinking about this, I am reminded of an analogy from Body psychotherapy. Totton (2003) identifies three main models of Body psychotherapy, i.e. the differing rationale and methods for how a Body psychotherapist chooses to work with his or her clients. He sees distinctions between what he identifies as three models. These are: (1) the adjustment model; (2) the trauma/discharge model; and (3) the process model (Totton, 2003: 53-61). I shall say a bit more about each of these three models and how they can be seen as analogous to approaches to meditation and embodiment, and you can see whether these coincide with your views and assumptions about meditation.

Firstly, the adjustment model implies that there is something to be fixed, in order to return to a state of 'normality'. Translating this into a meditation context would be about seeing meditation as a corrective treatment or a set of techniques to 'put right' something about your experience and/or practice. Meditation might be seen as something you *do to* your body and mind, in order to become more 'normal' and 'healthy' and better able to practise. This model assumes that meditation is some sort of cure; if you can only train your mind – and really crack this thing called meditation – the rest will follow like clockwork.

Of course, thinking in terms of the language of 'adjustment', there are very specific adjustments which can be helpful in setting up positive conditions for meditation. These might include working with your posture and adjusting that over time, as you become more flexible. Or perhaps adjustments in terms of the balances of practices with which you engage. Or perhaps making time to reflect on your ethical practice more consciously, giving you a clearer heart and mind for meditation. Adjustments like these can be very useful, as can reflecting on whether your overall rationale for meditating is that of adjustment and 'putting right', and whether this has changed over time.

Secondly, the trauma/discharge model. In Body psychotherapy this model is concerned with therapeutic release, in terms of healing the effects of traumatic experiences. In this Body psychotherapy model clients are likely to experience their own body as 'foreign' and somehow 'other', as a result of their reactions to early traumatic shock. They are likely to experience strong resistance to spontaneity and surrender, as they experience any excitation of energy as a further threat to their sense of stability.

Translated into a meditation context, you might see that you have a need for emotional release as a result of traumatic events which you have survived. You may have invested energy in alienating yourself from a full and whole experience of being a bodymind, keeping a 'safe' distance between you and these suppressed feelings and emotions. You might only be partially aware of the sense of 'otherness' in your experience (its purpose is to keep you 'safely' cut off, after all. The awareness work here is to at first notice, and then to be more at home with that sense of inner 'otherness' before emotional release can, in its own time, happen). Perhaps you resonate with this dynamic and can see how you have become more at ease with being a body over time, realising how cut off you were (and perhaps still can be), from a full, live sense of your embodied experience.

Here, the trauma/discharge model is about creating the conditions (in your meditation and reflections) to allow the acknowledgement and expression of emotions held or stuck in your body. This can gradually free you to become more conscious and aware of your embodied experience and fuller emotional expression, complementing your intellectuality. The processing of traumatic memories and events needs to be held carefully with kindness and mindfulness, and in relationship with others, to avoid re-traumatisation.

I am reminded strongly here of Guru Rimpoche – the legendary Padmasambhava, a great teacher of Buddhism and a mythical figure. In the eighth century, Padmasambhava took Buddhism from India to Tibet and Bhutan. He is infamous for his immense powers of transforming energies and subduing demons by showing them the radical magic of Dharma practice. In this way Padmasambhava can be a great source of inspiration and giver of courage, in facing and transforming your darkest demons, in the course of your practice.

Thirdly, the process model. This model, and the notion of process itself, has been a steady drumbeat of this book so far; noticing and being with what is happening in your immediate experience, just attending to, rather than intervening with a particular method or theory. I am reminded of Mindell's definition of process:

Process is information which comes to you in specific ways or channels such as seeing, hearing, moving, feeling, relationships and the world. Mindell, 1990: 17 (original italics)

Mindell's descriptions of 'channels' puts me in mind of the traditional Buddhist teaching of the four foundations of mindfulness, or 'satipatthanas' (see Analyo, 2003). These 'satipatthanas' are reminders of the importance of a full and whole mindfulness of: (1) the body and its movements and attitudes; (2) feelings (whether painful, pleasant or neutral); (3) thoughts; and (4) higher spiritual ideals (Sangharakshita, 1998: 155). These four foundations help to explore and cast light on your own process and experience of meditation and life, providing a rich working ground for reflection.

Process is being fully receptive to and in relationship with self, other and the world. Kurtz writes of this process in therapeutic terms: "If you want to help someone... turn the person inward towards experience. Don't turn them inward for explanation." (Kurtz, 1985: ii-iii)

Translated into a meditation context, drawing on the words of Kurtz, this model can remind you to turn inwards towards your experience, rather than turning inwards to seek explanations and interpretations. My teacher, Sangharakshita, says that there is nothing wrong with our experience; it is our *interpretation* of our experience which is the problem (Ratnadharini, 2005). Superficially, at least, the meditation practice which I have been taught in my tradition which is most obviously akin to this process-orientation is the one known as 'just sitting'.

In 'just sitting' you sit with as much awareness as possible in experiencing the moment. This practice might encompass both breadth and focus. For example, breadth might consist of an awareness of the noises and temperature of the room in which you are meditating. Focus might be more concerned with the activities of your bodymind. You might also notice your experience of being a body, compared to your experience of having a mind, and how you experience that, as you sit. There are a number of ways you can approach 'just sitting', but your primary aim will be to do as the name suggests – just sit and be aware! 'Just sitting' aside, you can choose to do any meditation practice anywhere between the two poles of a task or goal-oriented approach through to a process-orientated approach, depending upon your character, preferences and conditioning.

It can be challenging to communicate about meditation which draws on a process-oriented approach. In expressing something about your meditation practice to someone you can run the risk of fixing your experience, knowing well that words fall short of encapsulating rich, complex, human experience. Yet words are also so useful in sharing your experience with others.

This seems to be the constant dance between state and process in the 'spiritual' life. In this context, I mean 'state' as how you are at a particular moment in time, and 'process' as the ongoing, open-ended phenomena of your life (patterned by habits, volitions and circumstances) coming into contact with the universe. This dance highlights the creative tension between being with yourself and sharing a sense of your experience with another; the ongoing tussle between self and other in your dualistic perceptions of the way things are.

The three models can be useful in reflecting upon your current purpose in meditating as well as your relationship with meditation over time. They can also draw attention to how you see the nature of your bodymind, which we will explore in Chapter 3. In exploring your relationship with your meditation practice and bodymind I find it invaluable to remember the words of Sangharakshita: "There is really no spiritual life until the heart is also involved," (Sangharakshita, 1990(a): 37). In emphasising that a central challenge in the 'spiritual' life can be to develop the emotional equivalents to your intellectual understanding (Sangharakshita, 1990(a): 36), Sangharakshita explores the significance of coming into relationship with your emotionality as well as your intellect – your head *and* heart energies – in sustaining and deepening your practice.

Engaging the heart is essential in taking the leap of faith in practising a path of transformation. Making space for a growing warming dialogue between the energies of your head, heart and guts is invaluable as you explore your process in and out of meditation. I also find that engaging my imagination and intuition keeps my meditation in touch with the poetic, mythical and symbolic, which are vital to me in living everyday life. The more you can soften your expectations and desired outcomes around meditation – that sense of bargaining with reality – the deeper the effects of meditation: in body, speech and mind.

Reflections – meditating as process

Give yourself time to reflect, and sit in a place where you know you will not be disturbed. Agree with yourself how long you will spend on these reflections.

Begin by letting your mind turn to what you understand by meditation as a process.

Take a while to reflect upon how you view yourself in relationship to meditation. Do you view yourself as a meditator? Someone who struggles with meditation? Notice what comes to mind. How do others view you? What is your response to these views?

What useful and less useful habits have you developed? Are there things you habitually do in and around meditation, which limit your practice in some way? What specific changes might help with this?

What do you think meditation is? What sense do you make of the three models from Body psychotherapy, in terms of how you see your own tendencies and history and how you relate to meditation?

What do you celebrate about yourself and your meditation process, since the time you started to meditate?

During this exercise, remember to include thoughts, feeling, emotions, images, stories and memories that arise. You might also pay more attention to your dream life in engaging with these reflections.

Chapter 3

What is embodiment?

*Our body and mind are not two and not one. If you think your body
and mind are two, that is wrong; if you think that they are one, that
is also wrong. Our body and mind are both two* and *one.*
Suzuki, 1993: 25 (original italics)

I am appreciative of Suzuki for highlighting in this quote the
koan-like nature of understanding the nature of mind and the
nature of the body and how the two (or one!) interrelate. I
introduce this body-mind conundrum early in this book because
of its central importance, and as a 'live' starting point in looking
at your own embodiment. In the last chapter meditation was
explored as process. In this chapter embodiment is explored
largely as process, rather than as a particular end state. I have
chosen to explore the area of embodiment from a few particular
viewpoints, including looking at Buddhist views of psycho-
physical phenomena. Making sense of embodiment is a very
'live' area, with an upsurge of interest in research from neuro-
science relating to the nature of consciousness.

The bodymind koan
Making sense of the relationship between mind and body seems
to be something of a koan:

1   From a *theoretical* point of view, mind and body are simply
    two partial ways of considering the same phenomenon.
    What we call our mind can cause our body to move, for
    example, raising our hand. Conversely our body's sense
    organs condition experiences in our mind. Whilst body

and mind are often seen as distinct, these examples show their interrelated nature.

2   From an *experiential* point of view, there seems to be an inherent tension between mind and body, which it sometimes seems that no amount of re-education and awareness-raising will dissolve. In mainstream Western culture we tend to relate to mind and body as discrete entities – creating something of a tension between the two – conceiving of, and relating to them very differently.

3   The notion of body and mind is a koan, in the sense that the distinction has no final resolution. This koan is, nevertheless, a fruitful and rich question to ponder and reflect on in making sense of our own experience of embodiment (developed from communication with an email correspondence with Totton, 2008).

The long-standing Western struggle with the body-mind split touches upon a number of dimensions: philosophical, political, ethical, religious and scientific. It can be valuable to reflect upon whether or how this body-mind split has influenced our lives, views and approaches to our bodymind and whether those influences have been useful or detrimental.

In meditating it can be misleading and unhelpful to think in a polarised way, in conceiving of our body and mind as two separate things. One way to explore this is to meditate on the question 'Where is my mind?'. As you reflect upon this you are likely to realise more completely that neither body nor mind are fixed 'things', experiencing the riches of balancing body and mind, as Conger points out:

A body uninformed by mind and spirit may be given over to instinctual life or callous imitations, but a mind uninformed by the body loses its judgement and, in unforeseen and critical ways, blunders and retreats. Without the body, the wisdom of the larger self cannot be known.

Conger, 1988: 183

Making sense of embodiment

It is impossible to define embodiment in a concrete sense, given that embodiment is a live process. In talking to fellow meditators, it also became increasingly clear that different people's understanding of what embodiment means varies hugely. At this moment in time embodiment seems to me to be about the choice to be here in the current moment as fully as we each can be, with an awareness of bodymind. Embodiment is about a quality of being in which we are aware that we are a body with a mind and a mind with a body.

In terms of a more formal definition, the meaning of the verb *to embody* is according to the Shorter Oxford dictionary:

"... Provide (a spirit) with a bodily form." (Brown, 1993: 804)
and the definition of embodiment:
"The action of embodying; the process or state of embodying." (Brown, 1993: 804)

My friend's description of feeling embodied rather beautifully captures its spirit, particularly in its connectedness to the elements:

Being earthed, being grounded, and sensing my connection with the earth and the elements. When I am embodied, I experience myself in a state of harmony with the matter around me. I am an extension of that energy and matter and acting as a conduit – fully experiencing myself.

Embodiment as experience

To be awake, to be enlightened, is to be fully and completely embodied. To be fully embodied means to be at one with who we are, in every respect, including our physical being, our emotions, and the totality of our karmic situation.

Ray, 2008: xv

I have felt very embodied in my most blissful moments. I have also felt very embodied in my most grief-stricken moments. On days when I am struggling to connect with myself and my experience, my relationship with my body can feel robotic and cut off. You will have your own sense of when you feel more or less embodied, and how you experience this ebbing and flowing of embodied awareness, like an ever-changing tide. For Ray (in the quote above), to be "fully embodied" is tantamount to becoming fully awake and enlightened, highlighting the important – and far-stretching – role of embodiment in 'spiritual' practice.

Embodiment as process

How I use the term embodiment here is as a description of the processes of the body being experienced as integral to the mind and consciousness. One quality of embodiment reported by many meditators is that it tends to feel energising, in flow, giving rise to an alert sense of relaxation (rather like an upright, yet receptive, posture for meditation). Embodying is an unfurling, ongoing process, not an end state, or a fixed point. The extent to which you feel embodied can wax and wane – rather like the moon and its phases.

How you view yourself as a bodymind is also likely to ebb and flow between state and process. At times, you might be fixed upon identifying yourself with a particular state, at a moment in time. At other times, most likely when you are feeling more expansive, and in touch with loving-kindness, you might sense your current experience as one phase in a fluid process, with no discernable beginning, middle or end. The same is true in the process of being more or less embodied. There seems to be a constant universal dance or struggle between fixing yourself as being in a particular state and seeing yourself as one part of the billions of phenomena of the universe.

Awareness of this dance or struggle is central to understanding embodiment and the movement and expression of your energies. It can be easy to fix the notion of embodiment. I hear myself say, "My body is x," and then wonder if that's actually true and up to date, or whether it is my latest story or one of the more habitual stories of my life.

Embodied-relating

An essential dimension of embodiment (and existence) is being a breathing bodymind in relationship with the breathing bodyminds of other beings. It is a little abstract to try to make sense of embodiment outside of the notion of relationship; with yourself, others around you (human and other than human) and your environment. The six different character positions (known as: boundary, oral, control, holding, thrusting, and crisis) introduced later in this book are a prompt for you to look at your past conditioning around relating, particularly the life stages of birth, feeding and being nurtured, discovering your independence and autonomy, toilet-training and being shaped by other forms of rules, testing your will and assertiveness, and becoming a gendered, sexual being. As human beings our lives are dependent upon the lives of other humans – and their lives upon ours – yet it is possible to feel so alone and isolated, even when surrounded by others. Life is interrelated, yet we can often erroneously imagine ourselves to be a completely free (or imprisoned) agent.

Awareness of your embodying and disembodying

Focusing on your sense of when you are present and more embodied is likely to bring into relief – often quite immediately – a sense of when you are absent and least embodied. When you feel least embodied you might be acutely aware of your perceived separateness, which can reinforce your sense of 'I', 'me', 'mine', as opposed to feeling more interconnected. Understanding your less embodied experience is as rich as knowing when you feel your energies flowing and integrating. Through understanding the swing between these two imaginary poles: wholly embodied and disembodied, you can enter into fuller relationship with your body, honestly and congruently.

An example of the swing towards disembodiment from my own life is staying up web-browsing. Even when I know that I have to be up early the next morning, I am not deterred from searching the next webpage, the next webpage, the next webpage. I start to realise how tired I am, how scrunched up are my eyes, how my entire experience seems to be focused on my frontal lobe, how my fingers are locked in a typing position, how I am slumped forward in the chair, restlessly searching for and craving that all important piece of information.

As I notice these signs I gradually become more embodied; facing my experience and perhaps the slight shame of 'zoning-out' and wasting a few hours of precious life. I feel like I am coming down from a wave. I start to reconnect with a sense of my emotions, stretch my poor tense body and notice the after-effects of that restless searching. I sometimes notice a bit of existential unhappiness, that feeling of the sometimes seeming impossibility of being human and searching for the answer.

I am secretly hoping that this rings some bells and I am not the only occasional late-night surfer on the planet! Disembodiment and embodiment are not end states but different ends of a spectrum, or different points of a swinging pendulum. Sometimes – not always – the more cut off and disembodied we feel, the more likely it is that our energy re-aligns itself, moving into more conscious awareness and back towards greater embodiment. As your awareness of embodiment deepens you become aware of 'layers' in your embodiment, for example, reflected in your body armouring. You also start to see more clearly how your day to day embodying and disembodying tendencies are influenced by your lifelong patterning.

It may sound very straightforward to be aware of your disembodiment and embodiment. This may well be the case for some of you, which is great news. Becoming aware of how you might have cut off from your experience (going unconscious in the face of perceived or actual pain or threat, a habitual response from an early age) can be a painful process with which to re-engage. In tuning in to your processes of embodiment and disembodiment – rather like going deeper in your meditation practice – you face your views, fears and defence mechanisms. The sense of being cut off from being a body can also arise later in life, for a multitude of reasons, for example due to injury or other traumatic experiences. Although baby and childhood memories are enormously influential, you continue to develop strategies through life. You may have never experienced joy in your body for a number of reasons, and have little trust in the notion of the 'body's wisdom'. Each of you will bring your own associations and history to this theme.

A Buddhist view of psycho-physical phenomena

The processes of both meditation and embodiment can be viewed as a constant interplay between state and process. Approaching embodiment with an awareness of *both* of these, in parallel, is useful in practising Buddhism. Having looked at embodiment as experience and process I will now explore how two different Buddhist teachings throw light on what it means to be a bodymind. I shall do this through an exploration of the three 'lakshanas', the five 'skandhas', and a reminder from my teacher about the nature of the astral and subtle bodies.

One of the key teachings of Buddhism is that of the three marks of existence (or 'lakshanas'). The teaching of the three lakshanas is that conditioned existence is marked by impermanence, insubstantiality and unsatisfactoriness. By conditioned existence I mean that which is conditioned by the three traditional Buddhist 'poisons' of greed, hatred and delusion. When your response to your experience is coloured by greed, hatred and delusion, you are partaking in, and deepening, the habitual groove of conditioned existence.

Much can be said about the three lakshanas. I wish to focus here on impermanence and insubstantiality. Impermanence refers to how life is ever changing. Insubstantiality refers to how all beings and phenomena are devoid of a fixed, unchanging essence. It can be easy to think of ourselves as a fixed entity, rather than as an interconnected being, subject to the process of change.

The more I invite the conditions to live from an understanding of the three lakshanas, the more I live in accordance with life itself. Rather than constantly trying to fix, plan and bargain with reality I give myself the chance to be just a little more fluid, relaxed and receptive to what life brings. This does not just have the advantage of feeling more relaxed; it also means that my thoughts and actions are more likely to have a positive effect. I am drawn to living with more kindness and wisdom, thereby being more in touch with a greater ethical sensitivity. As a result of this I can rest more of the time in states of contentment, compassion and wisdom, rather than greed, hatred and delusion.

When I remember to reflect upon my experience in terms of the teaching of the three lakshanas, I feel somehow that I am really *living* life, yet the flavour of this really living is quite ordinary and simple. I also find it useful to reflect on the lakshanas with specific regard to the bodymind. To see our bodies as fixed entities, in a static state, is inaccurate. To identify ourselves as purely bodies or purely as minds is misleading. To deny that we have bodies, or at least live most of the time as if that were the case, is alienating.

Another way in which we can start to loosen our view of

things being fixed and substantial is to reflect upon the Buddhist view that all phenomenal existence and experience can be seen in terms of the five 'skandhas', (translated as 'aggregates' or 'heaps'). These 'heaps' are explained (and translated from Sanskrit) as:

> *rupa*, which means 'bodily form', anything perceived through the senses. The second skandha is *vedana*, 'feeling' or 'emotion' – positive, negative, pleasant, painful, and so on. Thirdly there is *samjna*, which can be roughly translated as 'perception': the recognition of something as being a particular thing, as when we perceive and label, say, a tree. The fourth skandha consists in the *samskaras*, translated by some scholars as 'steering forces', but better rendered 'volitional activities' or 'propensities' – acts of will and so on. And the fifth skandha is *vijnana* or consciousness: consciousness through the five physical senses and through the mind at various levels.
>
> Sangharakshita, 1999: 32-33 (original italics)

In looking at and reflecting upon the skandhas, we are reminded that a "person is not such a unified entity as at first appears" (Brazier 1995: 84).

So considering the three lakshanas and the five skandhas can encourage us to soften our perception of solidity and fixed views, in terms of what it means to be a bodymind amongst others with bodyminds, amidst the flow of universal processes. A further way in which we can reflect upon this theme is by exploring what Sangharakshita writes, in response to being asked about the nature of the subtle and astral bodies:

> the astral body would seem to be a subtle material counterpart of the physical body, intermediate between the physical body and the subtle body... From what I gather, it

would seem that you are born with an astral body, whereas the subtle body is more something which is built up as a result of spiritual effort... There is an aura at every level of your being...The main point is that you should not think of a body at any level as something absolutely discrete, as though there is an edge to your physical body beyond which there is 'non-body'. If you could see yourself through a sufficiently powerful microscope, you wouldn't be able to see where your body ended; it would just fade into a cloud of minute particles. The sharp edge you see with the naked eye simply isn't there – there is just a finer and finer aura extending out into space – and the situation is similar on other levels.
Sangharakshita, 1993: 137-138

Sangharakshita's comment, "The sharp edge you see with the naked eye simply isn't there," is useful in being aware of your self-view and conception of being a body. I appreciate Sangharakshita's reminder that we are a bundle of moving or shifting or blocking energy, phenomena and processes (made up of the afore-mentioned five heaps!) It can be easy to think of ourselves as having clearly-defined, discrete bodies held in and kept separate by the boundary of our skins; strengthening our perception of separateness in the way in which we relate to ourselves and others. This does not reflect the reality of our existence on a more subtle energetic level which stretches beyond our physical bodies. Relaxing this fixed view of ourselves enables us to live and relate more fully to ourselves, others, and the world.

Embodied practice?
Having looked at the relevance of some key Buddhist teachings it seems relevant to very briefly set the embodiment theme in a 'spiritual' cultural context: how meditation and Eastern 'spiritual' traditions have been received in the West. This is a

theme highlighted by Ray (2008) which is particularly pertinent here:

> The somatic teachings of Buddhism have not crossed the cultural divide that separates Asia and the West. This lack of transmission may be due to our own extremely disembodied state, in which we are literally unable to hear the call to embodiment present within traditional Buddhist practice.
> Ray, 2008: 45

Ray feels that meditation is often practiced as a sort of 'conceptual exercise' (Ray 2008: 46) in the West. With this in mind, I am also reminded of the notion of 'spiritual bypassing'. Welwood (2000) coined this phrase in noticing a tendency of Western 'spiritual' seekers to use 'spiritual' ideas and practices – like meditation – to "avoid dealing with their emotional unfinished business." (Welwood, 2000: 5) He cites the importance of letting go, grounding and awakening the heart in addressing this unfinished business (Welwood, 2000: 5).

Ray and Welwood's comments are useful reminders of the ongoing cultural influences upon age-old teachings and practices. Cultural factors will obviously vary considerably, depending upon your own background, ethnicity and so on, which will be explored in great depth in Chapter 7. Perhaps as a starting point it can be useful to look at the tendencies of the 'spiritual' tradition in which you have trained and practiced, in terms of how embodied and disembodied the approaches have been, and to what extent 'spiritual' bypassing has featured. In the following chapter, themes linked to 'why embodiment matters', will continue to explore how and why embodiment matters from a personal through to global perspectives.

Enlightenment must be lived here and now through this very body or else it is not genuine. In this body and mind we find

the cause of suffering and the end of suffering. For awakening to be an opening into freedom in this very life, the body must be its ground.
Kornfield, 2000: 178

Reflections – your immediate response to your bodymind

Create the time and space to notice and record your initial responses to your sense of bodymind. You might do this with words, images, a mind map etc. You might also spend time and energy noticing your felt senses in the moment. These are the sensations you notice in and through your body. As you notice felt senses try out being your own witness, rather than trying to analyse or interpret what's going on in your experience.

Do you see or sense or feel your body as:

- separate from your mind?
- a nuisance to be ignored?
- something which works for you maybe like your car or bicycle?
- a source of pleasurable experiences? Or painful and fearful experience?

Do you resonate with the notion of 'spiritual bypassing' in your own experience?

What images, thoughts, sensations and memories arise? Perhaps work with these themes in different ways: meditate and reflect on them, brainstorm them, and compare notes with friends.

Meditation: 'Tuning in'

Give yourself time to really attend to your embodied experience before, after and during meditation! If you are new to body awareness meditations, or tend to see body awareness purely as a means of relaxing before you get down to the 'real' business of meditation, spend 20 minutes before you meditate following this exercise. You might ask a friend to lead you through this meditation, in a calm, gentle way, or record yourself reading these guide-lines, so you can play them back to yourself as you meditate.

Posture: Sit or lie in a posture which supports your spine to be straight yet relaxed, and your head poised (on a chair, on cushions, or lying down). Make sure your legs are comfortable and able to support your weight. Support the weight of your arms and hands by placing them in a blanket which is wrapped around you, or by placing them on your thighs. Make sure you are as comfortable as you can be and able to sit or lie down for the time you have planned, bearing in mind any habitual aches, pains or injuries. If you need to move during the meditation, make gentle, mindful adjustments.

Begin by sensing your overall body shape and the weight of your body sinking into your cushions and the ground. Feel your contact with the earth and allow your weight to sink further and further into this sense of support. Feel the force of gravity through your body. Notice your inner tone as you start this meditation. Is it critical? Speedy? Slow? Calming? Invite a sense of gentleness and kindness as you talk to yourself through the meditation. If this sense of intimacy is an unknown experience tread patiently and kindly, as you might in approaching intimacy with another.

Purpose: Once you have a sense of your body, bring to mind why you are meditating at this time. What's your purpose? Give yourself as long as you need to contact fully this sense of purpose and motivation.

Elements and environment: Notice the conditions you

find yourself in, and your awareness of the elements. For example: the earth supporting the weight of your body and its earthiness, water and fluids in your bodily experience, fire reflected in the heat and temperature of your body and of the room you are in, air surrounding you and the pockets of air inside your body, the space you are occupying. Tune into your sense of consciousness as you rest in your reflections. Let your body breathe you as you turn inwards more and more deeply.

Exploring your body:
Imagine painting a picture in your mind's eye of the colours and concentrations of the energy you feel in your body. Or, instead, sense as fully as you can where you feel energised, tired, and dull. Kindly acknowledge your starting point as you are.

Picture or feel your spine as a magic cord, creating a sense of poise and balance between your top and tail: the sky and earth.

Start from your head and work your way down your body. Invite a sense of tender receptiveness in your internal dialogue. Notice when you deviate from this tone and bring yourself back gently. Notice areas of well-being and tension. Breathe into the tensions and let go where you can. Notice all aspects of the area of your focused awareness: front, back, insides. Don't forget a sense of your internal organs, muscles and bones.

Listen to your intuition as you scan. Enjoy sensations of melting, softening, relaxing, opening, and closing. Let in and let go. Notice any tensions or any sense of being clenched with a kindly awareness. Continue to breathe into areas of particular tension, inviting a sense of relaxation and well-being. Allow your limbs to soften, helping your body sink into the support of the earth beneath you.

Appreciate all that your body does for you in the course of everyday life.

Use your breath as a way into your embodied experience. Let it follow its own course and rhythm and trust that it knows what it is doing. Follow your breath for as long as you wish.

Gradually take time to move gently from this exercise to the next task of your day. Or perhaps move into a different form of meditation practice, whether that is walking or sitting.

Chapter 4

Why embodiment matters

We have assumed that our lives need to have no real connection to the natural world, that our minds are separate from our bodies, and that as dismembered intellects we can manipulate the world in any way we choose. Precisely because we feel no connection to the physical world, we trivialize the consequences of our actions.
Gore, 2000: 144

Embodiment, connection and sustainability

Living with an awareness of connection and interconnection is integral to aiming to live sustainably in the twenty-first century. Realising connection is also a vital part of 'spiritual' practice – including meditation. We are each part of innumerable systems and sub-systems (of nature, human life, and other than human life): a complex web of connections and ecosystems. By living sustainably, I mean living a life that meets our needs without compromising the needs of future generations to meet their needs (see UNWCED, 1987) and avoiding exploiting their environment.

The spirit and practice of connection is invaluable in meditation. Meditation is about connection: with ourselves, others and the focus of the meditation. In sitting to meditate we connect more fully with our experience and purpose, being an embodied bridge between the inner and outer worlds. There are many tangible ways in which meditation is about connection. The mindfulness of breathing and other breathing meditations are ancient practices encouraging us to recognise and realise connections. At what point does 'the air' become that which we each call 'my breath'? How does this highlight our views about self and other, inner and outer? We share the same air, so our breath links us invisibly to all the other breathing beings on the planet. Each breath links us to the beginning of our lives and to the last breath we will breathe at some unknown point in the future. As we breathe we have the chance to sense the connections – and lack of connections – between the different parts of our bodies.

Connection is also a strong theme of loving-kindness practices. The practice of loving-kindness is about opening to a positive intention towards ourselves and others, and being receptive to interconnection in a live and lived sense. Similarly, the traditional Buddhist meditation practices cultivating and opening to the 'four sublime abodes': loving-kindness, compassion, sympathetic joy, and equanimity, are invaluable in terms of providing the juice for effective connections with ourselves and others. So we deepen our ability to connect with others (or to be clearer about what limits that connectivity) if we engage fully with any form of meditation practice.

Understanding and practising connection starts with ourselves as we understand more fully our embodying and disembodying dynamics. We might start by acknowledging our habitual sense of disconnection from being a body. Or we might see that we are habitually over-identified with our body in a particular way. As you read about character positions later in the book you are likely to make further connections between your past conditioning, your current thoughts and actions and the effects upon yourself and others. So I am referring here to connections on many different levels of experience, from what seems like the intensely personal through to the 'big' questions about self, other and world.

On a micro level, being connected with others is important in helping us to sustain our practice and the way we engage skilfully in living life. Living in a sustainable way is inherently linked to the macro picture of global connection and sustainability at this critical time for the planet. It can be easy to think that we are too insignificant, small, or unpopular to make a difference. This is unhelpful thinking, generating feelings of low self-worth or guilt, and undermining our potency in feeling that we have anything to contribute in life.

I am reminded of the bodhisattva ideal here. A bodhisattva is a being who longs to be enlightened for the sake of *all* sentient beings. In the current climate perhaps we are all called upon to be apprentice bodhisattvas, regardless of our faith (or no faith), in a multitude of ways, in terms of our awareness of how we are in the world (an awareness of the quality of our 'beingness') and in terms of an awareness of the consequences of our everyday actions. Calling upon the qualities of the bodhisattvas – in whatever way that makes sense – can also provide vital backup resources in facing our pain and the pain so apparent in the world. As an apprentice bodhisattva there is always something we can do, whether that's a session of loving-kindness meditation, making someone a cup of tea or giving someone our full, embodied attention.

A tipping point?

In the current climate, disconnection can be more visible than connection in everyday experience. Reports of the levels of loneliness and social isolation seem commonplace, particularly in Western societies. Disconnection is also evident in the levels of disembodiment and the extreme polarities in the world. Whilst billions of humans and animals die on the planet due to politics, trade policy and mismanagement of many forms, others are starving to death in the name of fashion and beauty. In mainstream culture the body has become yet another commodity subjected to all sorts of diets, cosmetics, and dressed up at huge cost.

Somewhere between the agricultural revolution, successive waves of global imperialism and colonialism and the industrial revolution, some of us humans seem to have got the impression that we could be the masters and mistresses of our own universe, enshrined in the beliefs of the capitalist system. Money has become the form of currency which predominates. This currency has largely replaced the previous currencies of bartering, sharing, generosity, kinship, and skills-swapping in terms of how relationships are built and maintained in living breathing communities. These same global events, in parallel with religious, cultural and some philosophical ideas, have also meant that there has been an increasing body-mind split, perhaps most notably in the Global North.

In the recent past – recent in terms of the history of the planet – the prevailing philosophy underpinning life has been that we can buy what we want, with the promise that it will make us happier, more beautiful and so on. There has been little regard for the reality of the consequences of these actions and the 'life-style choices' of the consumer-driven age in which we live. We have collectively moved close to losing sight of our interconnection. For this reason, some talk of the current global situation as being at a 'tipping point' in terms of the survival of the human species.

There exists an extreme and obvious mismatch between reality – the world having finite resources, being in the midst of a severe loss of biodiversity, unprecedented climate change and the effects of an extraordinary polarisation between global wealth and impoverishment – and the capitalism of the Global North. It is a mismatch which we often ignore, deny or feel overwhelmed by, perhaps because of the sheer scale of the shift in consciousness and collective response which is urgently needed.

In parallel, the ways in which we as humans cause harm to ourselves and others, often in the name of politics or religion, are becoming more and more extreme and globalised. Thankfully there also seems to be a growing awareness of both the mismatch in perception between reality and the inherent design faults of capitalism and concern about the extreme polarity of views and harm caused in the name of capitalism. Whether or not the human race has tipped itself into a point of no return in terms of its own survival as a species is, of course, yet to be seen.

The Great Turning

What is heartening in the current climate is the growing tide of interest in more sustainable ways of living and being, in response to the extreme polarities of the global economy. This shift is thought of by some as "the great turning" (the term used by the eco philosopher and activist, Joanna Macy, since the 1970s, see Macy 1998: 17) or, in Buddhist terms, the need for a turning around at the deepest-seat of consciousness. The significance of this momentum is the fact that it is based on increasingly collective action; the coming together of people who want to live with a greater awareness of their environment and the future health of the globe and its people and species.

How and why is this relevant to the subject of this book? Because this 'great turning' encompasses the increasing self-awareness and deepening practise of 'spiritual' practitioners (as well as activists, politicians, campaigners, business people and others). 'Spiritual' practitioners from different traditions have a significant part to play in this deepening of global mindfulness and compassion. In meditating we re-enact connection with ourselves and others which will, in turn, influence the way we live our lives and our everyday relationships with those around us, and our environment: local through to global.

Connecting, healing, reclaiming

Moving to the micro-level: how and why do these global themes matter in the context of our practice of meditation and embod-iment? In my mind, there are several reasons. Here are a few:

Connectedness. The importance of realising our connectedness: with ourselves (and our various dimensions: conflicting drives, resistances, insights, etc), with being a bodymind, (rather than a body with a mind), with our heads *and* hearts (remembering that 'citta', the Buddhist term for mind, traditionally means heart-mind), to others around us (all beings – not just our human friends and family), to the local and global environments and ecosystems of which we are an interdependent part.

The more we realise this connectedness the more we feel at home in our own skin, freer to engage more fully with our meditation practice.

Healing. The significance of working to heal the splits: in our own experience and identity (for example: body/mind, self/other, past/present, love/hate, tame/wild), between our conditioning as a consumer and our fuller human nature (respecting all of life), between our 'worldly winds' concerns (which come and go as the wind comes and goes) and our earth-touching roots, with others humans with whom we are in conflict (personally, locally and nationally), and with other than humans (for example, animals which we have tamed and used for our own ends).

The more we create the conditions for this healing to take place, the more whole we will be as human beings. We will also have the potential to access all of our energies in our practice of meditation, experiencing our potency in the way we live.

Reclaiming. The need to reclaim: a sense of respect, love and awe for the earth and its processes (and, in turn, respect, love and awe for our bodymind and its processes), care and regard for other than human life, a sense of interconnection between our bodies and the body of the planet, a live connection with our spirit *and* matter, our whole sense of being a body, aside from being subjected to, and subjecting ourselves to conditioning and views about status, fashion, diet, cosmetics, surgery etc, and a good enough relationship with our bodies.

The more we can reclaim a sense a reclaiming of our earth-touching and sky-reaching embodiment, the freer we are to be more integrated, living a truer and more spontaneously ethical life.

A good enough relationship with our bodies

Connecting, healing and reclaiming each start with an awareness of our attitude towards ourselves and our bodyminds, as well as an awareness of our experience of ourselves in relationship with others. Looking at the nature of our relationship with our body is likely to throw into relief questions addressed in Chapter 3 about the nature of embodiment. What does it mean to be a body, particularly in light of the apparent body-mind koan and how we experience ourselves in terms of our identification with being a mind with a body, or a body with a mind? Reflecting upon cultivating a good enough relationship with our bodies can pose far-reaching questions about the nature of self and other, body and mind, past and present, and the nature of selfhood and how we make sense of that, neither denigrating our body, nor totally identifying with being a body above all else.

What immediately comes to my mind in thinking about this is a key turning point in the life story of the Buddha. At a time when the Buddha was very ill and weak, it is said that he accepted rice milk from a woman called Sujata. For a period of several years before this, the Buddha practised as an 'ascetic'. He undertook extreme practices such as meditating in the scorching heat of the Indian midday sun, sitting between two roaring fires, and fasting for extended periods, endangering his life in the process.

The rice milk from Sujata was incredibly restorative in helping him to return to good health, providing conditions in which he was again well enough to meditate and practise. Accepting the rice milk that day was the beginning of the Buddha emphasising the importance of the 'middle way' in approaching life. In this case, the middle way is between ascetic practice and a life of excesses; 'spiritual' laziness and self-obsession (the life of excesses perhaps echoing the conditions of the Buddha's formative years in the palace).

I appreciate this Buddhist teaching of the middle way with

regards to how it can help make sense of a good enough relationship with our bodies. The story of Sujata and the Buddha highlights a few important themes. The first is the nature of impermanence. The Buddha had deprived himself in the course of his ascetic practice, bringing himself to the brink of death. This reminds me of the fragility of the body. It can be hard to develop a good enough relationship with something which is so obviously subject to old age, sickness and death (the first three of the 'four sights' in Buddhism).

Admittedly, most of us might not have experienced this fragility of our bodies through practising extreme meditative practices – although perhaps some of you have. This story is a useful reminder of the fragility of the body, which is a useful pointer as to why we might find it challenging to develop mindfulness and kindness towards our bodies when it will, inevitably, get ill, get old and die at some unknown point in the future.

It is perhaps no surprise that there has been a Western philosophical split in the conception of mind/body and spirit/matter. The elevation of mind and spirit over body and matter seems to have seeped into several 'spiritual' paths and practices, and influenced what we value in societal terms. Certainly in more traditional Christian conceptions, 'spirit' has become prized over and above matter and body.

In some Buddhist circles there can also be a tendency to take a narrow view of the body because of its very transience. The German-born Tibetan Buddhist teacher, Lama Govinda, comments upon the negative attitudes towards our body and its transience:

Those who despise the body because of its transiency therewith only prove their mental immaturity. For them the body will become a prison, while to those who recognize the body as a creation and the visible expression of the very forces that constitute our innermost being, it becomes the temple of the mind. A temple, however, by its very structure reflects the qualities and functions of its indwelling spirit. A temple that houses a universal spirit must itself represent the universe. Govinda, 1990: 114

The second aspect of the story of Sujata and the Buddha which seems relevant here is about compassion. Sujata saves the life of the Buddha through an ordinary act of kindness. Following on from Govinda's comment about the universe reminds me of a comment from Sangharakshita:

We train ourselves to regard the bodies of others, and the whole material world, as no less important than one's own body and to be treated with as much care and consideration. The spiritual life is not all introspection and self-evaluation. Sangharakshita, 2003: 44

In giving rice milk to the Buddha, Sujata regarded the body and life of another. This act of compassion shows its far-reaching effects – what happens when we go beyond identifying with our own wants and needs (without disregarding them) in relating to others with compassion. In this way, compassion leads to greater relatedness (through everyday acts of kindness) which leads to a realisation about the nature of the universe. Developing a good enough relationship with our bodies might be about realising the universal nature of what it means to be a body and be a human.

This reminds me of an experience I had the day after my father died. Awash with my own grief, I remember walking around a very beautiful garden, bringing to mind all the other daughters around the world who were grieving for their fathers that day. The thought did not lessen the intensity of my own emotions, but it did open me up to a sense of connectivity with those other women in the universe, and to the truth – which for a moment or two seemed blindingly obvious – that people are born, they live, and they die.

Thinking about developing a good enough relationship with our bodies through compassion for others links to the earlier point about connection. In one sense, it is erroneous to think in terms of having a body as a separate entity. Because our body is contained by skin, it can be easy to think that we are free, independent, unconnected beings. In reality our bodies are a constant bridge between self and other, public and private, inner and outer (and our skin is in a constant state of renewal).

Reflecting and realising interconnectedness – as explored earlier in this chapter – is a helpful context for thinking about a good enough relationship with that which we call 'my' body. On a practical level, perhaps this is about navigating a middle way between respect and care, neither reinforcing our sense that we are our bodies and our body is somehow our ultimate essence (further adding to 'me-making'), nor denigrating our body, which is: "as futile and as much a distraction as pampering." (Pema Chodron, 2005: 141)

Perhaps we can reclaim a more whole sense of our bodies and nurture a sense of care in our attitudes towards our bodies, noticing our criticisms *and* our appreciation. It can also be useful to realise when we might be getting caught up in the needs and looks of our body. Developing a good enough relationship with our body might be something of an uphill struggle, particularly in the current climate. Perhaps this is part of a cultural legacy of seeing the body shaped by wild, untameable energies, compared to the cooler, more rational mental energies of the head.

An invaluable aspect of cultivating a stronger embodied dialogue is to engage the intuitive, poetic aspects of our natures, as well as the bits of ourselves which strive and plan. In that vein, I am reminded of some beautifully poetic words from Thich Nhat Hanh:

See your body's nature of impermanence and interbeing. Observe that your body has no permanent entity, and you will no longer identify yourself solely with your body or consider it to be a 'self'. See the body as a formation, empty of any substance that might be called 'self'. See your body as an ocean filled with hidden waves and sea monsters. The ocean may be calm at times, but at other times you can be caught in a storm. Learn to calm the waves and master the monsters without allowing yourself to be carried away or caught by them. With deep looking, the body ceases to be an aggregate of grasping... and you dwell in freedom, no longer caught by fear.

Thich Nhat Hanh, 1998: 177

Embodiment matters because it is one of the most fundamental ways of realising our connection with self, other and world: our breathing body existing on the living body of the planet. Cultivating a good enough relationship with our body is perhaps less about developing strategies, and more about reflecting on koans, for example: I am a body, but I am not my body. As we cultivate good enough relationships with our bodies and our responses to our personal histories, integrating our head, heart and gut energies, we experience more strongly the sense of connection with self, other and world. In feeling more connected with being a bodymind, in connection with other beings with bodyminds, we have a far greater chance of entering deeply into meditation, connecting with the present moment, our purpose, and the cosmic mystery of being alive.

Reflections – embodiment and disembodiment

The themes in this chapter span the local through to the global and might therefore take a bit more effort to unpack in your own experience. Set aside time when you have the space to reflect on your own sense of embodiment and disembodiment.

When do you feel more disconnected from and out of touch with your body? In which scenarios, settings and relationships?

What is your experience as you bring this sense of disconnection to mind? Recall as fully as you can this experience. How does it feel to recall this disconnected experience? What words, images, sensations, stories, memories come to mind?

What do you do to feel more embodied? Dancing, swimming, meditating, walking in the rain, making love, gardening? When do you feel most attuned with your bodymind?

What sense do you make of connecting, healing and reclaiming in your own experience of being a body? How does this relate to global questions and issues?

When do you feel most in touch with a sense of embodied 'flow' and the making of connections in your body? What does this feel like? When do you notice it most? Who are you with? Or are you alone? What are you doing? How does it feel to bring awareness to this sense of connection with your bodily experience, in the here and now?

Are the energies of your head, heart and gut free flowing or stuck? Do you focus on one at the expense of another?

Do you feel, overall, that you have a good enough relationship with your body?

Chapter 5

Understanding character positions

Introducing character positions

As you gain experience in meditation you notice patterns, habits and stories about your life. You might become more aware of how you relate to being a bodymind, and the way you habitually relate to others through a deeper understanding of yourself. This chapter explores the relevance and application of character positions. In the chapter which follows this one, I will explore the six character positions in depth. In Chapter 7 you will have the opportunity to reflect on your life conditioning and spend time applying what you have gleaned about the different character positions. In Chapter 8 the character positions will be explored specifically in the context of meditation practice.

The body of knowledge about character positions has been developed from an understanding of developmental stages from pre-birth to the age of about six or seven. The patterns and dynamics which contribute to the formation of armouring (both psychic and muscular) during these stages inform our view of ourselves, others and the world. Given that we have each passed through the developmental stages (birth, feeding, and so on), we are likely to have some resonance and empathy with the strategies of each character position. This is a useful aspect of character: it is grounded in the universal human experiences of what it means to be born and conditioned (even though that conditioning will, of course, vary, depending upon a wide range of influences).

In writing about character positions I am much indebted to the work of Nick Totton and Em Edmondson (Totton and Edmondson, 1988 and 2009). Here I will use the framework and formulation of the six character positions used in Embodied-Relational Therapy, with which most post-Reichian Body psychotherapists would agree (Totton and Jacobs 2001:44). The names given to the character positions are: boundary, oral, control, holding, thrusting, and crisis.

The heart of the descriptions of the character positions here are based on those found in Totton and Jacobs (2001), supplemented by what was taught on my training in Embodied-Relational Therapy. I have also drawn and reflected upon character in the context of my work as a therapist, which has given me a strong experiential sense of the influence of character armouring and strategies. I have found the following texts invaluable in making sense of the theory and practice of character: Totton and Edmondson (1998, 2009), Totton and Jacobs (2001), Kurtz (1990), Lowen (1994, 2003, 2005), and Reich (1990), the originator of character analysis.

Character and life themes

To give you an initial sense of each of the character positions, the main life themes of each are summarised as follows:

Boundary. Existential issues: feeling fully 'arrived' on earth and making safe contact with others.

Oral. Need: for support and nurturing from ourselves and others.

Control. Validation: the desire for independence and being influential in the world.

Holding. Autonomy: the need to self-regulate and to be valued, doing things in our own time, space and at our own pace.

Thrusting. Assertion: making our mark in the world in a driven, industrious way.

Crisis. Contact and attraction: feeling able to play, to choose, and to be ambiguous, rather than being defined by our gender and sexuality.

Character and conditioning

As well as arising from conditions we have experienced this lifetime, the character positions with which we resonate are likely to be associated with those volitions (or 'samskaras', introduced earlier) with which we arrived in this current life, from past lives. Character positions and their strategies influence the way we habitually respond to current life situations, ways in which we approach and express being a body, sometimes the physical shape of our body and how, where and when we feel, hold, and block energy.

Understanding character positions can give us a clearer sense of the strategies we adopted as a baby and child in response to different developmental stages and the people, interactions, events and circumstances in our early lives. These will be explained in detail as each character position is explored. Seeing these dynamics in the context of our approach to meditation and 'spiritual' practice can be illustrative in understanding our conditioning, views and what we find holds us back.

These influences are part of an intricate web of social, economic, cultural, political, religious, 'spiritual', technological and environmental influences. Consequently, there is a direct relationship between the health and well-being of each society and each individual within that society. Perhaps this is an obvious point, but one which is often overlooked in the current mainstream climate, where the main emphasis seems to be upon each of us individual beings existing as if in a sort of vacuum; free agents amongst other free agents.

The reality is that from conception we are part of a web of connections, conditions and phenomena. This web reaches back far beyond our conception this lifetime, in terms of family lineage and past life conditioning. We have the chance to be an active part of this lineage, in terms of how we respond to events and conditioning this lifetime. The strategies and armouring that we developed as a baby and child weave together karmic, genealogical and societal threads, each with their own powerful and unique influences.

The influence of character positions

In identifying the life themes with which we resonate, and in understanding how character formed, we can see how our habitual actions have perpetuated character patterning, even though the original threat is often no longer present. Our resistances are still doing their level best to defend and protect us. Perpetuating these old, often subconscious habits (the psychic aspect of character armouring) means that we further limit ourselves, following an old script and staying with a model of ourselves that we have outgrown. In parallel, the muscular armouring we experience will also influence our approach to life, our energy, and our experience of being a body. It is worth remembering that:

> The characterological and muscular armour, as Reich constantly emphasised, must not be understood as two separate processes, but as two manifestations operating at different levels.
> de Marchi in Boadella, 1976: 341

It is an interesting question as to why and how we found one or more particular developmental stages particularly challenging compared to others. It is also a complex question, linked to parenting, cultural rules and norms, and the particular habits with which we personally arrived in this current life. This is an evolving area – the body of knowledge linked to character positions has been researched and developed over the past one hundred or so years by three or four generations of doctors, psychotherapists and body workers. Here character positions are presented in a way which highlights the possibility and creativity of life and practice, discovering the riches of our bodymind in understanding ourselves, others, and the world in which we live.

Outgrowing old views

The character strategies we developed when we were young made sense at the time, in response to perceived or actual threats. They often make less sense in the present-day, now that the original threat has most likely subsided. Yet we continue to approach life and embodiment from this patterning of character, given that it worked for us as a strategy in our early years and is embedded in our body memory.

Exploring character positions can help us to identify how and when we are acting from a character which we have outgrown and which no longer serves its original purpose. Once we have seen and sensed how different aspects of a character position might limit us, we begin to consciously create the conditions for the emergence of greater awareness in choosing how we now respond to challenges and recurring life themes. This might involve shedding old skins and having the awareness to recognise and let go of out-dated views and models of ourselves.

Please bear in mind that character is *not* a rigid theory, a justi-fication, or a way of blaming yourself (or others) or patholo-gising. Sometimes a starting point in the process of outgrowing old views is facing and letting go of the view that there is something inherently wrong with us; something which needs 'fixing'. Character is not about reinforcing insecurities, it is a:

> subtle account of *individuality in relationship*, and of the strategies and defenses used to preserve individual freedom – and the price paid in doing so.
> Totton in Staunton, 2002: 19 (original italics)

Character and relatedness

In developing character patterning and armouring we were instinctively doing what we thought was best to survive and thrive. Gaining a stronger understanding of character positions in our own experience can show us how the rich tapestry of our life relates to the more universal experiences of human life: our conception, growing in our mother's womb, being born and arriving on earth, coming into contact with our parents and/or carers, feeding, understanding our influence and independence in the world, learning about written and unwritten rules and norms of behaviour, learning whether and how we can assert ourselves and becoming a gendered being in the social world.

Whilst we grow up in a unique set of conditions, we share the experience of living through these developmental stages and becoming part of a web of relationships in a specific cultural context. In exploring character for ourselves we can make sense of how the personal meets the universal; how we exist in the world and see more fully how others exist in their worlds, rather than purely in relationship to us.

Reflecting upon character can be clarifying and encourage us to cultivate compassion for ourselves and others. We can make more sense of the differences and similarities between ourselves and others. This might be particularly the case in terms of the people who have most influenced our lives, events we have lived through, situations our parents and ancestors survived and the times and circumstances into which we were born. These can provide invaluable insights into understanding our related place in the world and that of others.

Character and practice

Character offers the potential to support a deeper understanding of our embodiment and the different stories of our lives. Understanding character in this context throws light on our deeply engrained habits and feelings. When we hear ourselves say "That's just me, that's the way I am," it is likely that we have caught the tail end of a fixed self-view about ourselves, reinforced by the patterning of a particular character position.

Hearing this view is likely to be particularly relevant if we are meditators and 'spiritual' practitioners; curious about our deep patterning, and perhaps wishing to identify and loosen our fixed self-views.

This is relevant to those of us who are Buddhist practitioners, seeking to understand and dissolve our attachments to our strong ego-defining sense of 'I' and the process of 'me-making'. This strongly engrained sense of 'I' limits the scope of our inter-connection and freedom to live life unconditioned by the three traditional Buddhist 'poisons' of craving, hatred and delusion. Loosening our grip on 'me-making' activity and softening our fixed views of ourselves and others is remarkably freeing. Here, I mean freeing in the sense of setting up the conditions to live in a more spontaneous, kind, authentic, ethical and open-eyed way in living our interconnectedness. Understanding our process of embodiment through the lens of character positions can deepen our everyday understanding of the centrality of conditionality: the important Buddhist teaching that all things arise and fall in dependence upon conditions:

> The Wildmind... is not afraid to look suffering in the face. It sees pain as an opportunity to learn, not a sign of failure. It embraces impermanence because in a fixed universe there would be no freedom.
> Bodhipaksa, 2007: 5

Character as process

The more we are aware of the particular character positions which have shaped us, and how the positions might work in conjunction with one another, the more we can create and invite the conditions – in meditation and life – to understand the limiting aspects of character. In time we can set up the conditions to go beyond these limitations. Looking at character positions invites us to understand ourselves and our process of embodying. There is no such thing as a cardboard cut-out sort of character wandering the planet. There are only us simple, complex, beautiful, messy human beings giving life a go. Whilst two of us with similar character position influences might recognise similar intra and interpersonal dynamics and life themes, the way these are expressed will be unique to each of our lives.

This reminds me of the wisdom of discrimination of the Buddha Amitabha, who is depicted as seeing everything as unique and distinctive, balanced by the wisdom of equality of the Buddha Ratnasambhava, seeing the sameness and equality in all things. Both wisdoms reflect the truth of what it means to be alive; simultaneously unique and yet equal. As you read I urge you to avoid 'shoe-horning' yourself neatly into one character position when the reality is that you are likely to resonate with different aspects of more than one of them, and their interfaces, given that you experienced living through each developmental stage.

In reading the explorations of each of the character positions you are invited to make sense of them in whatever way works for you. Depending upon which character positions sound familiar, you might find you have a preference for approaching this material in different ways: hearing, seeing, sensing, absorbing and analysing character positions. Follow your own style in exploring character inviting as much receptivity as you can, and giving yourself the chance to be surprised. The more you are in touch with your embodiment as you read about character, the more likely you are to understand the nuances of each of them.

Aspects of character positions: yearning, denying and creative

The introduction to the character positions in the next chapter is followed by a brief outline of the 'yearning', 'denying' and 'creative' aspects of each of the characters (Totton and Jacobs,

2001: 44). An explanation of these three different aspects is given below. As you read, bear in mind that it is very likely that you will resonate with more than one of these three different aspects of each character position, depending on the situation in which you find yourself, or in relating to different people. I say a little about the three different aspects below.

The yearning aspect of character positions

The patterning and dynamics of the yearning aspect of each character expresses the longing to complete the work that our bodymind needs to complete, linked to that particular position. This longed for work can be anything from learning how to feel more physically and psychically grounded, through to noticing our overwhelming longing to control people and events, depending upon the dynamics of the particular character in focus. The yearning nature of each of the character positions – as the name suggests – is about our wanting, *longing* to fully realise the creative expression of the themes associated with this particular character position. For example, for the yearning boundary character position, this is a longing to feel as though we truly exist and are able to make safe contact with ourselves and others in everyday situations.

The denying aspect of character positions

The denying aspect is that part of us that is not prepared to accept the sense of limitation that this particular character armouring exerts. As a result, the denying dimension of each character can be experienced as a defended, more closed-down position, in that we continue to act from the more limiting aspects of that particular character position. For example, for the denying oral character position, this is a denial that we have any needs, and, in turn, a strong reluctance to ask for support from anyone else.

The creative aspect of character positions

The creative aspect of each character position is expressed and experienced when we have made inroads – consciously and unconsciously – in integrating character themes in terms of how we live, relate and communicate. The work we have done might have consisted of becoming more aware of how we were influenced by early experiences, with energy being blocked or limited in response to those experiences, and how we created the conditions to dissolve that conditioning.

This healing might have happened as we have engaged with body work, meditation and being in positive and reparative contexts and relationships. In the creative aspect of each character position we recognise the particular patterning and have a sense of choice in expressing ourselves creatively through how we live and interact. This brings a greater flow of awareness, choice, possibility and freer energy as we embody the positive aspects of that character.

I hope that you will get more of a flavour of each of these different aspects (yearning, denying and creative) as you read about each of the character positions in more detail in the following chapter. The aim of this chapter has been to set character positions in context. Lowen provides a reminder of how and why it is useful to explore character in our own experience:

> The primary nature of every human being is to be open to life and love. Being guarded, armored, distrustful and enclosed is second nature in our culture. It is the means we adopt to protect ourselves from being hurt, but when such attitudes become characterological or structured in the personality, they constitute a more severe hurt and create a greater crippling than the original one suffered.
>
> Lowen, 1994: 44

Chapter 6

The six character positions

The six character positions (boundary, oral, control, holding, thrusting and crisis) are explored in depth in this chapter. Each character position is explored in terms of significant life themes, the associations with particular areas of the body, interpersonal dynamics and areas of challenge and working edges. A brief explanation of the yearning, denying and creative aspects of each character follows the main body of information about each character position.

The boundary character position

Existence and safety are significant life themes for us as boundary characters. In our appearance, energetic expression, and actions, we will sense an uncertainty as to whether or not we are welcome or belong (Kurtz, 1990: 43). This links to the fact that the boundary character position starts to form either before or during birth, or in our earliest phase of life, which gives that uncertainty deeply felt roots. Uncertainty is something of a boundary watch word – uncertainty about existence, reality and making safe contact with ourselves, others and what is happening around us. Those of us patterned by the boundary character will return to the same questions, consciously or unconsciously: Do I exist? How do I exist in a dangerous world? Am I real? What is real? Our life work (and the work our body needs to complete) is to make sense of what it means to fully arrive and to be as present as we can be in the world.

Our deep-seated boundary fears of taking our place, and making contact, mean that our relational strategies are likely to be about:

minimizing self-expression and emotional contact with self and others. The pattern reflects threats to survival and the core material will organize perceptions, feelings and actions around a theme of inescapable danger. Kurtz, 1990: 43

When there is any perceived threat to our safety (for example, walking into a roomful of new people), we might experience an inward or outward sense of freezing, or making ourselves invisible, energetically 'leaving' our body through disappearing into our heads. As a result, boundary characters can come across as aloof, distant, slightly alien, overly analytical and logical (as we take refuge in our heads for the 'right' answer), and at times, strongly in touch with 'other'-ness or a mystical connection.

In this section, the boundary character position is explored in terms of energetic factors, relational factors, the influence upon physical appearance and exploring the eye segment block, which is the area of the body particularly associated with this character.

At least part of the character will be built upon a basic uncertainly about their own wholeness and reality, and every crisis of life will be experienced as a threat to *being*.
Totton and Edmondson, 2009: 67 (original italics)

This quote gives a clear indication as to why boundary character energy can seem somehow withdrawn: because of that underlying uncertainty around wholeness and reality. This withdrawal of energy can give us the appearance of being ungrounded, or undergrounded. We give a strong impression of living in our heads, a perceived 'safe escape' from the world and relationships. Kurtz calls the boundary character 'sensitive/withdrawn', with the name giving an immediate energetic sense of this character position (Kurtz, 1990: 47).

As a result of life events witnessed by those of us influenced by boundary strategies, there is likely to be a central theme and questioning around boundaries, physical and otherwise: "'Do I have any? Where are they? Is it safe to let anything come through them?'" (Totton and Edmondson, 2009: 67-68) There is likely to be an internal sense of "Where do I end and where do you begin?" Those of us with this character patterning are likely to feel some confusion on a basic energetic level as to whether or not we are contained by skin. Not only do we feel this lack of containment and wholeness, there can also be a very real terror of fragmentation and of falling apart. The seeking, sometimes piercing, expression in our eyes as a boundary character shows our deep longing for and simultaneous fear of contact with ourselves and others.

Given that the key theme of the boundary character is focused around existence and feeling welcomed and belonging, it may come as little surprise that when our attempts to make contact with others are experienced as too scary; one of our key strategies is to 'float off', away from the contact that may be experienced as too invasive. Obviously we do not disappear physically, but energetically we are long gone, leaving a sense of relational vacuum.

Lowen gives a detailed description as to how those of us with boundary character conditioning experience an overall lack of unity and wholeness in our body. He comments on the important energetic separations between our body and our heads, with a splitting of our body at the diaphragm, a disunity of the trunk and the pelvis and disassociations of the extremities (Lowen 2003: 338).

Lowen continues to point out how those of us with this patterning maintain only a tenuous connection in terms of our body-mind unity, particularly when we become cut off, or disas- sociated from our body. He gives the example of how we use our body a little like we would use our car, in a mechanical, utili- tarian way (Lowen, 2003: 334). We may often feel cut off from a more live, immediate, kinaesthetic sense of our body in the moment. In this process, those of us with this patterning lose, what Lowen calls, the body as a 'bridge' between our inner reality and the material reality of the outer world (Lowen, 2003: 334).

This perhaps helps to explain why boundary characters can appear to almost look a little 'alien' and 'other'. As a young baby we did not have the energetic sense that we were actually present in our body, let alone relating to, and accepted, by other earth-lings, as that information was not forthcoming from our early environment. Energetic interruptions around pre-birth, birth and our early life on earth mean that – in an energetic sense at least – we are still finding a way to arrive fully, to feel sufficiently safe to make contact with others, and to be present in our body.

Kurtz gives the example of Mr. Spock (from the popular US television series *Star Trek*) as an example of the traits of this character position: "Mr. Spock, though fictional, is a good example; the person's movements may be stiff and/or awkward, bodies are often thin and very tense and tight." (Kurtz, 1990: 43) It is not uncommon for those of us with strong boundary character patterning to take up some form of physical activity, often quite early in life, as a way of trying to become more co-ordinated, to feel less awkward or clumsy, and perhaps intuitively to feel like our movements (and psyche) are more joined up.

The formation of the boundary character position is strongly linked to armouring in the eye segment block. One reason for this link to the eyes and the upper head is because we seek immediate contact with those around us from the moment we are born, a natural human survival instinct. We need to receive the message – energetically, verbally, and through touch – that we exist, that we have arrived, and that we are welcome and safe. Without feeling these messages via the eyes (literally, being seen and able to see our carers) and skin, as a baby we become incredibly confused and distressed as to whether we are actually real and whether we have been safely delivered. Given that this is a pre-verbal stage, or an in utero stage of development (Smith, 1985: 92), this confusion can be experienced extremely acutely. As a newborn baby it was impossible for us to give verbal expression to these intense feelings, at a time which is such a seminal and formative point of life.

As a baby we are so dependent upon others that we need mirror-like validation to know that we are real and safe. If we did not experience this, through sufficient eye gazing contact and soothing touch, we may well have developed the sense of incompleteness of the boundary character. Our bioenergetic system will then be built around an underlying, pre-verbal uncertainty about our relationship with reality and the reality of ourselves and others.

A strong theme will be the importance of really seeing and understanding, having a well-functioning 'lens' on life and anchoring ourselves through our eyesight, vision, and visions. This will be influential in how we relate to others. Lowen writes about the experience of others, coming into relationship with the boundary character:

> You do not feel that he looks at you or that his eyes touch you, but that he stares at you with seeing but unfeeling eyes. On the other hand, when his eyes focus on you, you can sense the feeling in them; it is as if they touch you.
> Lowen, 2005: 59

As a boundary character, we continue to seek the warmth of contact and safety through our eyes; yet that contact is also the thing we fear most. Part of this patterning is characterised by a strong, seeking, or distant, faraway look as we lose contact and disappear into our mind's eye. When contact is not made, or perhaps made and experienced as too invasive, our eyes have a "typical *faraway* look of remoteness" (Reich, 1990: 430, original italics). By being able to 'really see', those of us with this patterning will be able to assess our safety, often with a sense of hyper-vigilance, knowing whether it is okay to be present in a situation.

What is going on energetically for the boundary character, relating to self and world? We have seen how those of us influenced by this position can at times seem out of touch with reality, operating in a survival way. This may or may not be obvious to those around us, given that we can 'float off' but still appear to be physically present and make the right noises. Lowen talks of the ego of the boundary character being a "will without an I." (Lowen, 2003: 333) In other words, we have a weaker ego strength than other characters, a less defining sense of 'I', 'me', 'mine', because of this uncertainty about existence and being welcomed. Having said that, we have a sense of will, but it is likely to be more akin to a: "power to do things and not as a power of thought." (Lowen, 2003: 333)

Those of us with armouring shaped by the boundary character position can have a rich inner world, often shaped by deep analysis and intuition. What we find more threatening is the stepping out to relate to others. Lowen points out how: "Ingrained characterological attitudes of 'I won't' and 'I can't' are missing" (Lowen, 2003: 333) from this character position. Because we are already uncertain about our connection with reality and being present, there is not the same need to fight this reality or to see it as unfair or unjust (as we might if we were also influenced by the oral character position), which we will look at in the next section. As a boundary character our main work is to come to terms with existing and arriving, daring to connect more fully with the material world, and full, sustained relationship with a grounded sense of self and other.

Under extreme stress, those of us with boundary character patterning can have strong survival functions and be highly attuned to external forces and energies. This attunement has a number of consequences. It means that boundary characters:

"responds to affection immediately and directly but just as immediately will he freeze in a situation which he feels is negative" (Lowen, 2003: 334). In relationship we may:

> find ourselves seeing other people as feeling angry or afraid when that is what *we* are feeling, or perhaps we let other people's ideas take us over and dominate our own sense of things.
>
> Totton and Edmondson, 2009: 68 (original italics)

There can be an extreme sensitivity to the psychic and 'spiritual' realms. When this is grounded and integrated, it can be a gift; when it is a heightened undiscriminating awareness it can be unclear and confusing. That confusion may be experienced as a deep uncertainty about who or what is real, and what is inside and what is outside.

In looking further at the interpersonal dynamics of the boundary character, one striking thing is that we expend quite a bit of energy in avoiding contact and relationship. As Fenichel points out: "The emotions of these persons generally appear to be inadequate... They behave 'as if' they had feeling relations with people." (Fenichel, 1945: 445) Or as Kurtz says: "Feeling like strangers in a strange and dangerous land, these people strongly limit self-expression and contact with others," (Kurtz, 1990: 43) Lowen goes on to point how our aggression can be " 'as if' aggression, it is 'put on' as a matter of survival," (Lowen, 2003: 332) rather than being a more integral part of our experience.

In summary, the themes that pattern boundary character's inner working are safety, being welcomed and making contact. These are reflected in our need to see (and our corresponding eye segment armouring) and in our tendency to live in our head, unable to inhabit the life of our body because we are still working towards a sense of wholeness. Our lifework is to bring more awareness in weaving a greater sense of head and body unity, for example, by starting to pay more kindly attention to those situations where we disappear into our head. We might breathe and ground ourselves as we feel the familiar pang of uncertainty about what is inside or outside, as we pick up cues from the energy and atmosphere around us; vital information to which others are oftentimes oblivious. In relationship, our work will be to feel safe and present in making authentic contact with others.

Yearning boundary character position

Those of us influenced by the yearning boundary position are likely to feel a strong sense of yearning for contact with others, yet an equally strong feeling that contact will further threaten us. This can feel like an impossible place in which it feels unsafe to be alone and out of contact with ourselves, and even more unsafe to seek contact with others. We are likely to have a strong sense of being less real – or 'differently' real – compared to the other humans we see around us.

I often notice this with therapy clients who have had a lifelong sense of not being real or belonging, in quite an existential way. This feeling and fear may have been reinforced by the criticism and derision of others telling us that we were (or are) weird or eccentric. Relationally, we are likely to experience a push and pull pattern of fear between the longing for others to help us feel more real and present and the intensely felt fear that this contact will create further damage and put more distance between us and the reality in which we see others living.

It is important for boundary characters to understand and make sense of the world. We are likely to approach life with a strong sense of quest; really *seeing* what's behind life: the big questions. We may approach this quest intellectually (like the academic in the ivory tower or scientist in the laboratory) or in an intuitive, equally intense questing way, seeking information from many dimensions of experience (perhaps inspired by the mystical or archetypal dimensions). An important life theme will be experiencing ourselves fully enough, and being present enough, so that we are able to engage with life. This safety may be provided by the context in which we live or by an internal sense of creating the conditions to know we are now safe enough to be present.

Denying boundary character position

If we have been shaped by the denying boundary character position it is likely that we are still largely removed from a wish to be present in the world. Those of us patterned by this aspect of the boundary character are likely to believe that we can only trust our own reality, and no one else really exists, in terms of dependability and relationship: others are aliens or fantasises, existing in the 'no-go' zone of relationship. As a result, we are likely to retreat into the infinite, cosmic resource of our own mind and our rich and vivid imagination. One of our core themes as a denying boundary character is that we will seek to 'complete' ourselves alone, avoiding having to make contact with others, or as little as possible. We are likely to choose to stay as far as possible away from the world, literally or metaphorically. We will prefer to live far away from the threats of making contact with others, in the safety of our imagination and clear-thinking, logical mind.

Creative boundary character position

The creative boundary character position is exemplified by those of us who are in touch with a truly infinite web of realities, with information and flows of energy at every level, from the intellectual, logical, energetic and mystical. We will have an amazing capacity to notice things, think, analyse and synthesise information from a multitude of sources. We will draw upon logic and inspiration as we connect with others, and with all phenomena: revealing and creating patterning and making sense of the whole. We will have the capacity to stand back from the fray of relating to and making contact with others, without having to stand outside and withdraw. In a 'spiritual' context, we are likely to feel a certain ease in facing the 'big' existential questions about life, death, the nature of self and so on. In fact, we are at home in this realm, supported by having a clear-thinking mind and sensitivity to accessing information from a multitude of information channels.

The oral character position

"The person may feel there is some tragic flaw in them that makes them unacceptable to others and there is likely to be an inner rage about being abandoned." (Kurtz, 1990: 44)

Moving down the body, to the area of the mouth and jaw, the key issue for the oral character position is that of need and support. The formation of the oral character starts at the stage of feeding as a small baby. Whilst this 'feeding' most obviously focuses upon food, it also includes our associations with our early experiences of other forms of nourishment (or a lack of nourishment). Our key concern will be around getting what we feel we need. Conversely, for those of us with more strongly denying oral patterning, there may be a strong denial that we have any needs at all, material or otherwise. Those of us with oral patterning may find that we are often concerned with getting enough, whether that is love, food, comfort, friendship. We will experience fear underlying our acute experience of lack; a fear which can 'cut to the quick', in terms of generating worry and fretfulness.

Those of us patterned by the oral character are likely to resonate – at times, at least – with the following:

'The world is empty and does not hold anything for me' may be equivalent to 'I am empty and cannot hold anything or anyone securely'.
Klein, 2002: 310

When we sense an imminent lack of nourishment and support we begin to feel deflated and in danger of falling into depression. The oral character is the character position which is most strongly linked to depression, as explored later in this section. Our sense of need is expressed in a range of ways. We might be endearing and gently demanding, right through to expressing ourselves in a bitter, biting and cutting way. Lowen reminds us that our experience shaped by this patterning can elicit:

> deep-seated feelings of loneliness, disappointment and helplessness. Lowen, 2003: 149

In this section the oral character position is explored in terms of energetic factors, relationship influences, and the influence upon physical appearance and an exploration of the jaw segment block, which is the area of the body particularly associated with this character position.

Similarly to the boundary character, our energy as an oral character tends to be held high in our bodies. The result of this is that we often feel and look ungrounded and disconnected from the earth. We might typically have a thin, soft, ungrounded body, finding it hard to sustain our energy. The oral character may be taller than average, tending to have fairly undeveloped muscles and a deflated chest area. Lowen (2003: 173) points out how those of us with oral patterning tend to have grown up too quickly, without sufficient nurturing. In seeking a stronger sense of being rooted, Lowen notes our body energy is constantly rising upwards, seeking the original nourishment which was not satisfied at a young age.

As a result of this the oral character can convey a sense of physical neediness and, at times, a strong sense of being deflated and close to defeat. This puts me in mind of a plant that has bolted; it has grown 'leggy' prematurely, rather than developing strong roots and having a slower, steadier pace of growth, fed with all the necessary nutrients. Those of us with oral armouring sometimes look as though we might easily fall down, as we are not well rooted (and do not feel well nourished) in our place on earth.

The oral character position is linked (more than any of the other character positions), to occurrences of depression, which are partly explained by the energetic patterning of this character. Those of us with oral patterning have a central theme of anxiety around support, nourishment and fear that there is not, and will not, be enough – love, food, care etc. Lowen (2003: 152) notes how our sense of disappointment and lack as an oral character is based around fear of rejection which is ultimately a fear of losing the longed-for loved object as a baby. In not getting our needs met we can fall back into this original depressive state, where the love object (originally the love and nourishment of our primary carers) is not available, giving rise to fear that we will never get the nourishment that we need to survive and thrive.

Because of this link between oral character patterning and depression, Lowen (2003: 145) suggests that the oral character shows more than any other character the dependence of what he calls the "psychic function" (how our mind and mental processes work towards certain outcomes) upon our underlying 'bioenergetic' processes (how and where our energy flows within us, as well as how energy interacts and is transformed between each of us, as living, breathing, organisms). Simply put, our mind and mental faculties are very much shaped by the flow, strength and vitality of our physically-experienced energy. This process and interrelationship is, in Lowen's opinion, most clearly shown in the pattern of falling into depression for those of us with oral character patterns.

The main physical area of focus here is the jaw and throat segment. The mouth and jaw are critical parts of the vocalising and feeding process. Totton and Edmondson (2009: 72) point out how an oral block can interfere with the full pleasures of activities such as drinking, eating, kissing, singing and talking, and those of us who have adopted oral strategies will either overindulge in these things or find difficulties in engaging with them in some way. They also point out that in the jaw segment there is often held back anger, a desire to bite, which when suppressed can give rise to underlying hatred (2009: 35). The needs that were unfulfilled as a child can exist under the hard blocking of the jaw, particularly anger, disappointment and resentment about not being fed, nourished and supported.

The oral character search for getting our needs met will be a central theme in our relationships with others. This will be our default position, in the way that an infant at first looks to his or her mother or main care-giver to do this. As an oral character we seek love, security, and care, looking for our needs from others rather than recognising that much of the time as an adult we need to learn to fulfil our own needs. This is the crux of the dynamic between self and other for the oral character position; fully realising that we can and do learn to meet our own needs without falling into the familiar cycle of depression.

Realising this is likely to be something of a breakthrough for those of us with oral character patterning. It will also mean that we start to see how much we load on to our relationships with others, in terms of seeking our needs outside ourselves, albeit that this habit is out of awareness much of the time. This was an understandable expectation as an infant, when we were completely dependent upon our carers. This expectation becomes more problematic as we get older, as it is unlikely that anyone experienced being perfectly nourished, although not everyone experiences it as problematic to the extent that they develop oral armouring and oral character strategies.

What is most important for those of us who resonate with the oral character position is to become aware of the level of our expectations in coming into relationship with others, experiencing the world through a 'hungry' position of needs and wants. That which the oral character:

> holds out as love is experienced by others as a demand for love... his attitude in the love relationship is not based on the adult pattern of give and take.
>
> Lowen, 2003: 153

The more we can create a balance between meeting our own needs, accepting support from others, and meeting the needs of others, the more balanced and positive will be our relationships with others.

It can be illuminating to understand how this works interpersonally. In terms of the central oral theme of getting what we need, those of us with oral patterning can get into a challenging cycle of feeling the acute anxiety and fear of not feeling like we will get 'enough': love, care, whatever defines this 'enough'. The nature of this 'enough' is almost immaterial. We have seen that what motivates us is a deeply experienced sense of focusing upon getting whatever it is we feel we need. Because of past experiences of not getting what we needed (perhaps mostly strongly experienced at a pre-verbal stage), we feel fear and reticence in making an effort to reach out for what we want or need. This can become a vicious circle – we avoid reaching out for what we need because we fear being disappointed. In avoiding reaching out we can fuel the self-fulfilling prophesy that we rarely get what we need. As Lowen says:

> (the oral character) hopes to get what he wants somehow without reaching for it; in this way he can circumvent the feared disappointment.
>
> Lowen, 2003: 154-155 (author's brackets added)

Our lifelong strategies as an oral character will have been a constant search for the place, person, event, and situation who, or which, will meet our needs, relieving our fears about our inability to survive alone. What we seek in relationship with others will be intricately tied up with our oral needs and a very real sense of imminent or ongoing deprivation. We can experience a very tangible fear of abandonment and fear of loneliness, strengthening our sense of neediness. At other times in our lives this empty, lonely search for nourishment can tip into bitter resentment and moaning about life's injustices. Those of us with oral patterning have a strong reluctance to accept the fact that life is, at least at times, a struggle, because accepting that would feel simply overwhelming.

In summary, patterned by the oral character position, our central themes will hinge around need and support. If our lifework as a boundary character is to accept that, yes, we *are* here on earth and we *are* real, our lifework as an oral character is to accept that we can survive, partly through being supported by others and partly through meeting our own needs. As an adult our work is to realise that we are able to cope, meet our own needs, as well as looking for significant, caring others with whom we can experience the giving and taking of support.

Yearning oral character position

As a yearning oral character we long to feel well supported and nurtured. More often than not we act from a sense of neediness, dependence and complaint. We may experience strong feelings of isolation, depression and powerlessness. We often see ourselves as being too weak to meet our own needs, let alone those of others, with a common complaint that others continually fail to support us.

I am reminded here of a traditional Buddhist image – the Tibetan 'wheel of life' (see Sangharakshita, 2002: 13-29). This ancient image depicts a circle divided into six segments, with each segment relating to a different realm of existence. These realms can be seen as reflections of our own internal states at different times. One of the realms is the 'hungry ghost' realm, in which beings are always searching for food and sustenance, they keep searching and searching, but they are never satisfied, regardless of how much they eat and drink.

Denying oral character position

As a denying oral character we are incredibly self-reliant and avoid looking to anyone else to fulfil our needs, at all costs. As Kurtz says, our central strategy will be to:

> organize perceptions, feelings and actions around themes of challenge and going it alone.
> Kurtz, 1990: 44

It will not occur to us to seek support for anything in our lives. We will push ourselves to achieve things and face challenges alone. This constant striving – a lone quest – bears some surface similarities to the actions of the thrusting character position. The main difference is that as a denying oral character we are seeking to prove to ourselves that we do not need anyone else to survive. As a thrusting character we act like this driven by a more explicitly competitive, out-to-win driver.

We might resonate with the denying oral character position if we tend towards being overly self-reliant and individualistic, finding it impossible to ask for anything from anyone, fearing that this would compromise our self-sufficiency. This over self-reliance is likely to stem from our experience (or lack there of) of nurturing and feeding having been intolerable as an infant. Our resulting strategy is to 'go it alone' and deny having any needs. This character position can lead us to become very isolated, concealed behind a façade of 'I don't need anyone or anything'.

Creative oral character position

Patterned by the creative oral character position, we will have a big, healthy appetite for life, secure in the knowledge that life now provides what is needed enough of the time to stem our continual fretting. This sense of abundance – rather than the abject need of the yearning oral character – can lead to a sense of potency here, in caring for ourselves and others. Some of us are likely to take centre stage as extremely eloquent communicators. The taking centre stage aspect of the creative oral character position is shared with both the creative crisis and control character positions, as we shall see later on in this chapter. For the oral character, taking centre stage is linked to our desire to gain interest, attention and love. The association between the oral character and speech is a reflection of the nature of oral armouring being based in the jaw and mouth area. This expression can give voice to a whole range of themes, for example, recognising inequalities in society around us and adding our voice in countering social injustices.

The control character position

The key issue for the control character position is that of validation. As a control character our armouring and strategies developed as we took our first wobbly steps towards independence in our interactions with our significant others. Our exploration of our growing independence is likely to have seen us wanting to influence and shape, testing our new discovery that we were an independent being. In developing control character patterns, our playful testing and experimentation would have been denied or thwarted. We received the message that trying out our independence was unacceptable. This denial of our experience would also have obscured our sense of understanding the other person in those interactions.

As a result, as an adult we find it hard to experience ourselves just as we are. This will particularly be the case with regards to our independence, for fear that we will again experience that sense of being invalidated, rather than being accepted or affirmed and allowed to feel okay as a separate being. We will feel a strong impetus to be in control, shaping and organising those people and things around us, including how we present ourselves to the world. One friend with this conditioning says of herself:

> I step outside of myself to see how I'm doing. Is how I appear acceptable to myself? Am I portraying myself as I wish to be portrayed?

For whatever reason, our early carers may not have had the capacity to engage with our play and experiments, dominating our early attempts at trying out our power or giving us the message that this experimentation was not acceptable or right. Feeling the force of this message enough times, we are likely to have internalised the sense that being independent and testing out our power was simply not okay. Consequently we felt invalidated, with an accompanying feeling of a lack of control and the development of armouring (physical and emotional) around our heart area.

In feeling unable to experience our sense of independence in a straightforward way – for fear of it being denied again – we are unable to sense and respect the independence of others, and their reality (lest they overpower us). Those of us patterned by this character position have therefore developed the strategy of being in the world through staying in control of ourselves, others, and events, so we constantly feel our impact, affirming to ourselves that we are valid and acceptable beings. As a control character we will want to make our mark in order to be present in the world.

Kurtz calls the control character position two different names, the first 'tough-generous' and the second 'charming-manipulative', which gives a clue as to the strategies of this character position. He goes on to point out that: "both types try to control others; one uses power and generosity, the other uses seduction and charm." (Kurtz, 1990: 45) As a control character, we may adopt one of two main strategies: a charm offensive (seductive, magnetic, and charismatic), or telling others what to do (and how and when to do it).

In this section the control character position is explored in terms of energetic factors, relational factors, and the influence upon physical appearance. The chest segment block is explored, which is the area of the body particularly associated with this character position.

Our energy and armouring as a control character is concentrated in our chest and heart area. In the yearning and denying manifestations of this character our energy will be more congested, or split off, in this area rather than energy flowing and moving more freely, as patterned by the creative control character position. The heart and chest area is the important meeting point for energy rising up from our contact with the earth, and down from our connection with the sky. In terms of control character armouring: "The jammed up heart of the control character usually manifests physically as a sense of bulkiness and inflatedness in their upper torso." (Totton and Edmondson, 2009: 74)

In terms of physical appearance, Lowen (2003) and Totton and Edmondson (2009) point out how we might tend towards having smooth features and perhaps flabby, rather than strongly defined, muscles. Totton and Edmondson (2009: 40-43) observe how the chest and heart need to be open for us to express strong feelings and to feel expansive emotions. When those of us with control character armouring feel defensive we become more tightly closed around the heart, attempting to protect and defend ourselves and our deepest feelings. This strategy is not only to protect our hearts, but also to make us appear stronger (and, quite literally, more 'armoured') then we inwardly feel. As the armouring of the heart segment starts to dissolve:

We sense ourselves as strong, real and formidable, without being aggressive or having anything to prove: a *soft* power, which asserts our need for contact yet is able to deal with hostility or coldness.

Totton and Edmondson, 2009: 42-43 (original italics)

Our main intention (consciously or subconsciously) will be to hide our true intentions, keeping our tenderness and fallibility well under wraps. We will aim to gain influence in our relationships either through being tough (perhaps a form of 'tough love') or wonderfully charming. This patterning can play a strong part in our energetic sense and force field. Kurtz observes: "The surface behaviour will feel 'slick' and elusive. The person usually has a desire to be in a position of power or authority." (Kurtz, 1990: 44)

In relationship with others, those of us patterned by the control character position tend to have a definite, at times overbearing, presence, as we remind others of our influence. What characterises our style of relating tends to be choosing either one of two strategies:

We can seek to *dominate* other people, by physical force or by force of will; or we can seek to seduce and *manipulate* them... Underlying either strategy is a fundamental lack of belief that other people are *real*, that they have feelings and needs, experience pain and pleasure.

Totton and Edmondson, 2009: 74 (original italics)

What underlies this unrelenting need to control and shape? Our driving force is a deep fear that we will once again feel invalidated and not seen for who we really are. In our independence not being accepted and validated we became confused as to whether we had influence in the world, and whether we could accept the influence of others without feeling overcome ourselves. So this confusion stems from the experience of not being allowed to experiment creatively and safely with our own sense of independence interacting with the power of others, in the dance of learning about how to be and how to come into contact with others at a formative point in our lives.

As adults, those of us with control character patterning fear that this invalidation will happen again. To avoid this, we will have developed effective strategies to protect ourselves, notably through controlling others (and thereby being in the 'driving seat'):

> The basic uncertainty will be about whether or not one can have one's needs met in a straightforward way. The expectation is that others will use one's needs and vulnerabilities against one.
> Kurtz, 1990: 45

These strategies work inasmuch as they keep others at bay and seem to put us in charge. They start to falter when we want to make fuller, more authentic human contact, without the constant tension and exhaustion of having to be the 'mover and shaker'. The work for those of us with control character conditioning is to gradually allow others to be real, experiencing and shaping their own reality, without that being a threat to our own sense of reality.

This difficulty in showing vulnerability is a characteristic shared with those of us shaped by the thrusting character position (which will be explored later in this chapter), although it stems from a different developmental stage. Those of us with patterning from either of these character positions will find it hard to allow ourselves to feel vulnerable, let alone to share it with others – even those close to us. What we might see as personal 'weakness', others may simply see as straightforward human fallibility. Patterned by the control character position we fear that if we show vulnerability our experience will again be denied. We therefore feel we must remain in charge to prevent a repeat of feeling vulnerable and invalidated. Patterned by the thrusting character position, our fear in showing vulnerability is that we will be the 'loser' which, as a thrusting character, is tantamount to being destroyed, and facing the prospect of quite literally collapsing in a heap.

There are also similarities between the control character position and the crisis character position, particularly with regards to the seductive, charming elements of how this character patterning manifests. As a control character we can use our charms to get our own way, cajoling others to see things from our point of view. For those of us with crisis character patterning, seduction and charm are habitual ways of approaching contact with others. This charm masks our longing for – and simultaneously, our fear of – relationship. We approach relationship with charm, attraction, excitement and play, as a way of diverting attention from real contact with others. Whilst this seductive behaviour appears similar in both the control and crisis character positions, the origins of the development of these strategies are quite different.

Those of us with deeply ingrained control character patterning have been deeply wounded in the heart area. As we gradually feel more able to express our love, and as our sense of validation is not so externally-oriented, we will become less concerned with controlling others. Our façade of being king or queen 'pin' will also be less of a shield. Our lifework as a control character is to initially become aware of our armouring and strategies, and to allow ourselves to come into relationship with a softer sense of our potency and longing for influence. This is, of course, very challenging. As Totton and Edmondson remind us:

The control character with their locked-up heart is wounded

in a very deep place. But always, the wound represents the potential for growth: people whose energy focuses in the control position are people whose energy focuses in their heart – people with 'big hearts', with the capacity for big expression.

Totton and Edmondson, 2009: 75

Yearning control character position

Those of us who resonate with the yearning control character position will recognise our intense need to be noticed and to be central to things, having our successes seen and validated. We will also be aware of a deep-seated desire to get others to do what we want them to do and our disappointment when they refuse to 'play ball'. However, to our dismay, our efforts to control others are often thwarted, leading to a strong sense of disempowerment. In this scenario we start to question the reality of others, when we realise that people are not validating our experience. We long to be in relationship on our own terms, with a 'real' person who will see how successful we are, and will not try to diminish our sense of ourselves.

Denying control character position

As a denying control character, we deny any interest in being around anyone else. Our general view of others is that they are weak, stupid and therefore a waste of time. "Why bother relating to weak and stupid people?" we might ask ourselves. We may go one step further and deceive and manipulate others. We might justify this to ourselves by thinking that others clearly deserve such treatment, if they are dumb enough to come across as so weak and malleable in the first place. Our priority is to focus first and foremost upon getting what we want, when and how we want it. We are likely to believe deep down that if we act with sufficient strength of character we have a right to whatever life has to offer, come what may. This might give us a rather 'puffed up' appearance, or energetic sense, as we attempt to appear dominating.

Creative control character position

As a creative control character we are likely to be a magnanimous, magnetic leader, big hearted and caring for those over whom we have power and influence. Most human beings have a lot of love to give and an almost universally recognisable human tendency is towards growth, wanting to love and be loved, acting from the heart. As a control character, the freedom to express this love and care is coloured by our prior experiences of just how much our energy and expression was blocked and limited. We are likely to be drawn to, and shine in roles in which we can be appreciated for our charm, charisma and ability to get things done.

The holding character position

Self-regulation and a sense of autonomy are the key life themes of the holding character position. The holding character is formed at the time of toilet-training and learning the rules dictating behaviour. This character position and its armouring would have formed when we were small children, feeling shamed or humiliated in connection with our toilet-training, timing, or 'making a mess'. Regulation, timing, rules and our relationships with others around these themes will be significant.

As a holding character we will be concerned with how we regulate ourselves, striving to get things 'right', and feeling a pressure to do things in the 'right' way. When all this pressure becomes too much we can feel very stuck. We can reach a point of near immobilisation and inability to act, which feels impossible in a very real, physical sense. This immobilisation may arise from inner confusion and frustration, or a sense of digging our heels in, in response to a pushy response from others, a pattern which is explored later on. We start to experience our own autonomy through re-establishing the relationship between our bodily sensations, natural rhythms and the ability to respond to these sensations in our own time, space and through feeling our sense of potency and wholesomeness.

In the rest of this section the holding character position is explored in terms of energetic factors, relational factors, and the influence of this character upon our physical appearance. The buttocks, thighs, and anus are the areas of the body particularly associated with this character position and its armouring. We might also be acutely aware of the tension in our shoulders (associated with feeling the 'weight of the world').

Those of us with holding character armouring will often appear well grounded. We will tend to hold our energy low down in our bodies, which may well be reflected in our body shape, the regions of our body where tend to carry weight and our muscular development. Our sense of groundedness is in sharp contrast with the more 'sky-like' nature of those with boundary and oral character patterns, discussed earlier. The holding character provides a very different visual and energetic image, with a sense of being rooted to the earth, with a low centre of gravity.

The immediate physical and energetic sense we portray as a holding character is that of solidity, presence and being earthed – sometimes veering towards being stuck and rooted to the spot. With the oral character position I explored how there is a tendency to cyclical mood swings, with highs and lows. As a holding character, by contrast, we tend to experience anxiety to the point of immobilisation (particularly in an environment or relationship where persistent criticism is common place). As a result, those of us with holding character patterning can appear to experience a great deal of suffering – weighed down by this – reflected in the tension in our neck and shoulders. Theodore Reik described this aptly as: "like sinking in a quicksand where every effort sends one deeper." (Reik quoted in Lowen, 2003: 203)

Physically, we will tend to be wide-shouldered, or well-built, with slab-like muscular development. Our voice emerges from deep in our body. Our head tends to be set well back in our bodies, with our eyes sunk deeply in our heads, and with a thick neck. This physical stance can be particularly accentuated at times of experiencing shame, with our armouring showing the containment and internalising of energy. Kurtz gives the holding character the name 'burdened-enduring' (Kurtz, 1990: 45) which is useful in providing a very immediate sense of the physical and energetic stance of the holding character, seeming to carry the weight of the world. Those of us with this patterning also give a strong positive sense of being in touch with the goodness of our natural strength, natural rhythms and the ground. In the creative holding character position, rather than appearing stuck:

> Energy can be held and used; there is a quality of determination, patience, taking your time, working *with* the material world rather than against it – a willingness to get your hands dirty.
> Totton and Edmondson, 2009: 77 (Original italics)

As we have seen, the areas of the body where our armouring is likely to be most strongly experienced and pronounced are the anus, buttocks, thighs, and shoulders. Those of us adopting holding character strategies are likely to experience an anal block, which, in practice, means that our body is structured to contain and hold in energy, absorbing incoming energy so that it solidifies into defensive armouring in this region of our bodies. This links back to the time when we were given the deeply disapproving message that our natural bodily rhythms were unacceptable; so we assumed that we were unacceptable. The energetic block is linked to this message, internalised as a child and still experienced as inhibiting our natural connection with the rhythms of our bodily fluids, matter and functions. Our bodies, and its bodies of energy, may literally appear (or feel) 'squashed', matching our squashed experience as a child at the important developmental stage of toilet training and rules, which is particularly linked to the body and its matter.

In approaching relationship with others those of us with holding character armouring have a very strong desire for approval:

> They strive to please hoping that approval will bring love. In this, of course, they are constantly disappointed. We do not judge those we love and we do not love those that we judge. It is humiliating for an organism to feel that its security and acceptance depends upon its servility.
> Lowen, 2003: 200

This strong need for approval brings a sense of servility, combined with the underlying distrust that whatever we do will be met with further disapproval. This can reaffirm our original sense of shame and fear of further shaming. We are likely to hold a secret well of rage against rules, even though we are often so rule-abiding ourselves. This rage will be well concealed in the armouring of our anus, buttocks, thighs, shoulders and neck, with the rage itself being seen as 'nasty' and needing careful containing. Totton and Edmondson point out how:

> Anger turned inwards often becomes directed at the self in the form of guilt – this is the emotional correlative of physical holding, the person 'feels like shit', like dirt, worthless, foul.
> Totton and Edmondson, 2009: 76-77

In making contact with others we often give the covert, perhaps subconscious message, 'you can't make me'. In this scenario, the person to whom we are relating may have the experience of feeling provoked in a very subtle way. This strategy consists of seeking the longed-for approval of another, whilst holding a deep fear of impending disapproval. We look covertly for the other in the relationship to do things for us (echoing the pattern of our original carer being overbearing, 'for our own good'). We are likely to experience an internal tug-of-war around wanting to be pushed to take action, whilst simultaneously resisting, digging in our heels in a 'you can't make me' way – resenting feeling pushed, whilst still inviting it. This can be a very confusing dynamic to be around for those who do not understand the need of the holding character for autonomy and time and space in which to act.

The other aspect of this subtle provocative behaviour, which is particularly the case if we resonate with the yearning holding character position, is to subtly mess up everyday events, reflecting our original letting go being labelled as 'making a mess' as a young child. These events are often simple things such as being late, and forgetting things, concealing a very subtle and seemingly passive spitefulness emerging from the blocked rage of which I talked earlier.

The result of subtly but consistently messing up everyday events is eventually met with the frustration and disapproval of others. We are subsequently likely to feel disapproved of, energetically affirming the status quo of our character armouring and reinforcing the 'you can't make me' vicious cycle in relating to others. This pattern is often playing out behind a façade of smooth niceties, in an effort to be liked, even if the net result is frustration all round. To sum up this complex and at first, seemingly contradictory dynamic, Lowen says:

> We are dealing with a personality in which indirection, ambivalence and manipulation of situations are the character-istic qualities.
> Lowen, 2003: 209

To summarise, our central themes as a holding character are the dynamics of holding in versus letting go, and fear of showing ourselves, lest we are once again shamed. These are the themes that pattern our inner dynamics, concentrated in our pelvis, chest, buttocks and anus, neck and shoulders. Our lifework as a holding character is to become more aware of our natural rhythms, reconnecting with these on our own terms, rather than habitually fitting around the timetable of others.

As Kurtz (1990: 47) points out, those of us influenced by this character position want to feel an absence of pressure, responsibility and guilt. We wish to be free to do things for ourselves and to express ourselves fully and freely. Energetically, this integration is likely to be realised through our having the conditions to have the time and space to re-acquaint ourselves with our natural rhythms and our experience of those rhythms. From this greater sense of ease, rather than anxiety and distrust, comes a sense of us being grounded in our own strength and potency.

Yearning holding character position

Those of us patterned by the yearning holding character experience very strong urges to make a mess, let go, and bring our insides out, giving ourselves the chance to be admired and to feel recognised and affirmed. These strategies seek to release blocked and stuck energy – resulting from our energetic containing and holding – particularly in the lower part of our bodies. We are likely to sabotage anything that gets in the way of this yearning (the aggressive aspect of the passive-aggressive patterning). We also express a lot of energy in our attempts to break free from the constricting aspects of containment; breaking through and disrupting whatever gets in the way of that process.

Denying holding character position

The denying holding character is expressed in over rigid, habitual, regulated attitudes to time, systems and lifestyle in general. Those of us who recognise this particular aspect of the holding character will understand the mix of inner tension and anxiety. We are also likely to recognise the constant pull of what we should be doing next, rather than being able to be more present in the moment. This leads to a rigid adherence to following rules, timetables, and procedures in order to be rewarded and to feel a sense of worth. The denying holding character is likely to express passive-aggressive strategies in frustrating others by inflicting rules upon them or by boring and frustrating them through long-winded expression and rigidness of character. Living life 'by the clock' will also be expected of others. This is the aspect of the holding character position which is associated with the archetypal bureaucrat.

Creative holding character position

If we resonate with the creative holding character we have the grounded ability to stand in our own potency and strength and act from that basis. Inwardly this reflects our sense that we are now free to follow our own rhythms and values, appreciating the stuff of which we are made. We may be the 'salt of the earth'; in touch with our sense of earthiness, not afraid to serve others – in the best sense of the word – and to get our hands dirty through hard work. This sense of service means we are capable of working in a very committed and dedicated way, working systematically and with perseverance. There can also be a strong sense of honouring the rhythms of nature and respect for the rhythms of other beings, in a very grounded, wholesome and kindly way.

The thrusting character position

As thrusting characters we are very much focused upon asserting ourselves. We assert our needs and wants at all costs, in order to feel alive and present. The development of this character position is linked to the time when we were toddlers, finding our way in the world and experimenting with our sense of rebellion in figuring out – quite wilfully – what was and was not up for negotiation with our carers. In being met with either strong disapproval, punishment, or, even more extreme, a thrusting parent who did not welcome our assertiveness, armouring will have formed around issues of assertion and punishment.

The thrusting character position is formed when this natural experimenting with rebellion is seen as 'bad' and 'wrong', or when our parent or carer crushed our will:

> built into their character from then on will be a quality of *hatred* and *revenge* that subtly flavours everything they do.
> Totton and Edmondson, 2009: 78 (original italics)

Thrusting characters tend to frame situations and events in terms of winners and losers and achievement and failure. Those of us shaped by the thrusting character position will find it incredibly challenging to allow anyone else to win. We will find it virtually impossible to allow our soft, human vulnerability to show in relationship with ourselves and others, seeing this as a sign of weakness and, from the point of view of our childhood experiences, potentially dangerous.

In this section, the thrusting character position is explored in terms of energetic factors, relational factors, and the influence upon our physical appearance. The areas of the pelvis, thighs and lower back are explored, which are those areas of the body particularly associated with the thrusting character position.

In terms of body armouring, as a thrusting character we will experience a pelvic block against softness and the expression of vulnerability. Our physical appearance is likely to be athletic, with a strong appearance and well-developed muscles; a mesomorph-type body. Very often those of us influenced by this character will have a body in the shape of a 'V', with narrow, powerful hips and wide shoulders, accustomed to carrying premature responsibility. Our energetic presence will concentrate upon achievement, will power, pushing ahead and 'type A' behavioural characteristics (Friedman, 1996). Reich points out how thrusting characters tend to come across as:

> self-assured, sometimes arrogant, elastic, energetic, often impressive in his (or her) bearing.
> Reich, 1990: 217 (author's added brackets)

The pelvic block against softness and other aspects of thrusting character armouring would have formed at the age of about four or five. At this point in our lives we could walk, explore and had started to experiment with our sense of independence and testing our wilfulness. Typical events linked to testing out this assertion may have been play time and bed time. When our natural sense of experimenting with our assertion was met with strong judgement or, more influentially, the sense of being crushed by a thrusting parent, the thrusting character armouring would have formed. An important emotional aspect of our armouring as a thrusting character is the quality of revenge that flavours our actions, based on the early blocking of our natural assertion.

In portraying a sense of assertion we make our presence known, appearing upright and rigid, with an air of determination and wilfulness. To not be constantly upright would be tantamount to our admitting defeat and a risk of being destroyed by others. We are likely to experience injury and illness related to stress due to this need to be so upright, 'on top' and in the lead.

Our life work as a thrusting character is to allow ourselves to soften, to contact our sense of vulnerability and not to have to approach every aspect of life as a challenge to be overcome or an obstacle to be destroyed. This will not be easy work. Firstly, it is deeply unsettling for us to let our guard down in any situation, in fear of once again feeling crushed. Secondly, we tend to turn those we encounter into potential or actual opponents, the moment that they challenge any aspect of our behaviour. There are very few contexts in which we are challenged by others because we can be fearsome in our interactions, so that others tend to defer to us. If we can learn to start to turn inwards, then we can start to find out find more fully 'who's at home' and to see the effect we have on others.

We may, however, be forced to look at our behaviour and reflect on our character when we face physical problems. Then we face the fact that we, too, have a human, fallible body just like everyone else. For example, we may start to learn to meditate at the recommendation of our doctor to help with high blood pressure. Or we might come to see a Body psychotherapist as a last ditch attempt to figure out why we are unable to rid ourselves of chronic back pain, which has become debilitating, threatening our much-valued sense of uprightness and peak performance.

At first glance, those of us influenced by the thrusting and control character positions seem very similar in our shared wish to control people and events. The difference here is that as a control character we feel valid and alive so long as we are in control of others. As a thrusting character our assertive drive gives us a sense of being alive, so long as we can dominate others in our lives. As a control character we do not automatically feel the need to put others down – so long as we have an overall sense of control. As a thrusting character we generally frame events and relationships as a game or war with two sides: winners and losers. It is, of course, important for the thrusting character to be on the winning side (and, preferably, the team leader).

As others fight back in response to our provocation, our aggression will be inflated, as Reich reminds us:

> He (or she) is felt to be totally aggressive and provocative by those who are not in control of their own aggression.

Reich, 1990: 218 (author's added brackets)
The more others fight back, the more determined to fight and win we become. We secretly respect those who can meet us head-on, without aggression, modelling a full sense of being human, embodied and not afraid of our wilful presence. Such a person might also command our respect by demonstrating that it is also okay to be human and have human fallibilities and weaknesses, without being at the mercy of these fallibilities. In the long run it is only through learning to meet others and accepting them for who they are that we can start to experience real contact with others, rather than always being the winner, the high achiever, and the one with adrenalin coursing through our veins.

An added physical dimension here is that the thrusting character can find it physically uncomfortable to cry, as the movement of crying is antithetical to the rigid armouring of this character position (Lowen, 2003: 264). Even in private moments of vulnerability, we are likely to find that our bodies are armoured in such a way that means that tears and the release of soft, heartfelt emotion is deeply uncomfortable, as well as challenging our need to be upright and on guard at all times, regardless of the cost.

In Kurtz's schema of character strategy, the thrusting character relates to what he calls the 'industrious-overfocused' character. Kurtz points out how our main strategies are to work hard, keep going, let nothing distract us and take refuge in action (Kurtz, 1990: 43). He goes on to point out that, for the thrusting character, the missing core experience is:

to be loved, appreciated, just for who you are, freedom to relax and play. Kurtz, 1990: 47

This lifework of learning to be who we are, to relax and play is important work if we are to experience real contact with others, without having to turn interactions and relationships into a game with winner and losers, however overtly or covertly we do this. We can gradually soften our drive to get revenge against our original carers, the first people to crush our sense of natural, curious, assertiveness.

I have explored how we are likely to find it very difficult to engage with this pelvic block to softness, to show our vulnerability and to allow ourselves to be human, given our defences and strategies. What adds to this difficulty is the fact that in much of mainstream life a thrusting approach to life is affirmed, particularly for men, most notably working their way up the high-powered, corporate career ladder. For those of us who find ourselves with thrusting character patterning, there is little obvious incentive (at least, in mainstream worldly terms) to engage with and become more aware of the more negative, limiting and damaging aspects of our behaviour.

Of course, there are those of us who express our thrusting character strategies in a much more creative way, achieving a great deal for the good of many others, rather than just for our own sense of achievement and need to conquer. As those of us with thrusting character armouring start to recognise our own strategies and defences, it is likely that our assertive, upright need to achieve will be expressed more creatively. As Totton and Edmondson remind us:

> The creative side of the thrusting character is its energy, drive, courage, ambition, physical and mental élan; its willpower and discipline.
> 2009: 79

Yearning thrusting character position
Those of us who recognise ourselves as having been patterned by the yearning thrusting character position are likely to relish feeling successful, strong, risk-taking and defeating those who stand in our way. We are very proud of our successes; in fact,

they define who we are. We seek ever harder, more stimulating challenges, whether that is a higher mountain to claim, a stronger conflict with a work colleague or even pushing ourselves crazily hard in meditation, striving to break through hindrances and obstacles in a wilful way. The downside of this constant working and fighting is that we rarely relax or let go, which can have a detrimental impact on our health and our ability to be in non-combative relationships with ourselves and others.

Denying thrusting character position

The denying thrusting character lives life looking out for number one, living from a 'dog-eat-dog' outlook on life. Here our connection with our vulnerability and feelings are tenuous, which means that our ability to empathise with others is also lessened. As a result we despise, ridicule, and humiliate others, particularly those of the opposite sex. We find that life generally holds little enjoyment; in fact, if we see someone else enjoying themselves, we are likely to respond through attack, verbal or physical, covert or overt.

Creative thrusting character position

Those of us who resonate with the creative thrusting character love stretching our abilities. We aim to do the seemingly impossible, thereby pitting ourselves and our skills against the world – loving the buzz. I am reminded of the mountain climbers in the film, *Touching the Void*, climbing an impossibly difficult mountain in far from optimum conditions, driven by the compelling nature of stepping into the unknown of such a challenge. Life is only worth living when we know we are trying our absolute hardest. This may well be for a worthwhile cause, and we will enjoy basking in the success following that achievement, before moving quickly on to the next challenge. We seek out and carve out opportunities to live life fully at every possible moment.

The crisis character position

Making contact and relating are our key themes as a crisis character. The areas of the body linked to the formation of this character position and its armouring are the thighs, pelvis, chest and eyes. Those of us patterned by crisis character patterning can give perplexing energetic messages; we are desperate to make contact, yet we are terrified to do so, with our energy sometimes whipping into an inner frenzy. This character formed at the time when we were taking on all that it means to be a boy or a girl; our gendered identity in the world. This is a complex process and a delicate time in the development of any individual, in terms of how conditioning extends from the familial through to the social, political, economic, religious, and cultural. Attraction is an important theme; as Kurtz reminds us: "The basic uncertainty will be about whether or not one is interesting, attractive or wanted." (Kurtz, 1990: 46)

Some of our key life questions will be about contact: how do I make contact and stay safe? Can I make contact without it being sexual? Can I be myself, without having to be attractive and/or entertaining? As a crisis character we often become overexcited or bewildered in the face of making contact with others. This is such a familiar sense to crisis characters that it may not be identified as overexcitement or bewilderment, but simply the familiar deep down 'fizz' and fear which accompanies approaching others.

Those of us shaped by the crisis character position can become more relaxed in making contact through giving ourselves the chance to be really quiet and still, rather than through constantly entertaining, playing and performing for others. For some of us it is only through fully and deeply experiencing this quietness – which is likely to be deeply unnerving and challenging at first – that we realise how fear, mingled with excitement, underlies much of our motivation and shapes our life energies.

In this section the crisis character position is explored in terms of energetic factors, relational factors, and the influence upon our physical appearance.

Staying in a similar region of the body to both the holding and the thrusting characters, the particular areas of the body connected with crisis character patterning and armouring are the pelvis, thighs, and chest. The atmosphere we create around us tends to be one of high charge, with a strong underlying fear. We tend not to be very well grounded, but instead prone to sudden bursts of energy, emotional expression and the dramatisation of events. Our eyes will also play an important part in this dramatisation and our ability to attract and enchant. Whilst the thrusting character position is characterised by a pelvic block against softness, the pelvic energetic block for the crisis character is against opening and surrender. This block to surrender is linked to the developmental stage at which the crisis character position developed.

This pelvic block developed when our early emerging sexuality was met inappropriately. This inappropriateness may have taken many forms: deep disapproval, being told off for our nascent sexual feelings, or an inappropriate sexual response from the adults around us. This response tends to lead to feelings of overwhelm and immense fear linked to the development and expression of these early sexual feelings, which become ingrained in emotional and physical armouring. Those of us with this armouring fear opening up, or surrendering to, the felt sensations and pleasures in our bodies, for fear of feeling overwhelmed once more as we were as a young child (and perhaps, as an older child and an adult).

What happens for the crisis character around contact with others? When someone shows an interest in us we tend to experience a 'fizz' of excitement, alongside a corresponding 'freeze' of energy, as we feel unable to cope with this longed-for attention. Attention can induce a sense of terror. For this reason, our persona as an entertainer is a very effective distraction from revealing who we really are, aside from our dazzling performances and over-the-top drama. In providing surface entertainment we effectively conceal who we really are, hiding behind our exciting façade. What can be even more confusing in understanding this strategy is that we can even confuse ourselves as to who we are, hiding from ourselves behind the myriad of ways in which we face the world. This may be particularly the case if we also resonate with boundary character patterning, with the ability to 'tap into' different channels of energy. Life can become rather like a hall of mirrors.

This entertaining façade masks our immense – sometimes paralysing – inner fear. This behaviour – as well as our swiftly darting and dancing energy – is a manifestation of the armouring we developed as a defence strategy. Very often our bodies tend to attract attention in that we appear curvy, with a full build and a graceful way of moving. This body shape makes sense on the level of the crisis character being so fascinated by (and fearful of) attraction and relationship. We simultaneously find it disturbing to appear curvy and attract attention, yet our performing style attracts further attention. Our deep underlying ambivalence around real contact stems from our fear (linked to the pelvic block) of being overwhelmed as we were as a young child, during our first stages of sexual awareness. We also give a mixed message to those around us, almost as though we are play acting:

> In a sense they are pretending, but the pretence is an *involuntary* reaction to deep panic. The panic is completely rational in origin: dangerous and scary things *did* happen.
> Totton and Edmondson, 2009: 83 (original italics)

Energetically, one of our most noticeable and striking aspects is our constantly darting energy. The denying crisis character can portray a sense of somewhat muffled energy, often channelled into anxiety, appearing to be passive and numb in the face of sexual attraction from others. As crisis characters we have seen how our energy is constantly on the move, responding to the stimuli and excitement of the environment. This also means that we are often very sensitive, as we have developed a heightened awareness of verbal, non-verbal, energetic, visual and kinaesthetic clues to what is going on.

As a result of developing this heightened awareness of energies at work, as a crisis character we can appear to be – or to mimic – the other character positions: our energies constantly moving in response to the stimuli of different situations. The reason for this may be that we are genuinely influenced by the dynamics of other character positions. We also tend to be something of a chameleon, ready to adapt to our environment and to be experts in knowing the rules (implicit and explicit) and how to play with them (particularly if we are a creative crisis character). Because the central theme of this character position is relationship, we have an absolute fascination with figuring out the rules, roles and atmosphere in any given social situation. We are adept at observing, understanding, and mimicking (consciously or subconsciously) others in adapting to the environment. In knowing a culture and its rules we gain a greater sense of security in tuning into all the available cues. In this way we have the knowledge at our fingertips to know how to charm and entertain those around us, or when to run from impending danger, or perhaps when to take over and cause a stir or start a fight (if we are also patterned by the control character).

What makes the crisis position recognisable is its air of panic, of high charge. Everything is life or death. There is often either a theatrical exaggeration to the person's style, or a deathly stillness which is equally theatrical.
Totton and Edmondson, 2009: 83

The energetic aspect of this armouring is a readiness for energy to move, respond and dance, suffused with a sexual or sensual edge. On the surface, it can appear that our energy is very much flowing. Looking more closely, our excitement is intertwined closely with fear and anxiety. This relates to what has already been said regarding our attraction to making contact and relating. We tend to sexualise situations, relating in a flirtatious way. Lowen reminds us that crisis characters:

> will unconsciously seek situations which excite them and increase their inner charge. This is the bioenergetic explanation of their flirtatious behaviour.
> Lowen, 2003: 233

Those around us will be entertained, charmed, and even hypnotised by the chaos and drama we create. Kurtz calls this position the 'expressive-clinging' character, and points out that our strategies are to dramatise events and feelings to get attention and to avoid feelings of separation from others (Kurtz, 1990: 43).

Our contradictory dynamic of creating a drama and drawing attention to ourselves, yet at the same time wishing to keep people at bay, is very effective in maintaining our superficial identity as a fun-loving entertainer, seductress, or party planner, whilst concealing who we *really* are. Or at least, this is an effective strategy until such time when we want to make authentic, human contact with those around us, or they want to make contact with us, rather than contact based purely upon sexualised, dramatic excitement. Others can experience us as elusive and frustrating as they try to make genuine contact. The more others approach and try to make contact with us, the more we are likely to freeze or take flight, or do anything to avoid being present and authentic.

Reparative situations are those in which we are free to rest, free to be quiet, free not to entertain, not have to be sexual, and not to have to live with the persistent fear of being invaded or overwhelmed. It is in these situations that those of us with this character patterning will start to realise that we can receive the attention and care of others purely by being ourselves, as we are, without entertaining or creating a drama. We then start to realise that we have a choice in the matter, at least some of the time. Kurtz points out that the missing core experience for the crisis character is:

> freely given love and attention, not to have to struggle for attention, freedom to rely on relationships.
> Kurtz, 1990: 47

Yearning crisis character position

As a yearning crisis character we experience life as being 'too much', we experience ourselves as 'too much' and, as a result, we act in an over-the-top, dramatic way. Those of us with this character patterning will experience life as being full of exciting and terrifying events, people and phenomena. We often long for attention, but cannot quite keep still for long enough to be seen; wiggling uncomfortably as we stand in the longed-for limelight. It is particularly important for us to find out the rules in each situation we encounter, to help manage our sense of utter fear and panic. Once we know the rules, and have mastered them, we seek to break them in the most shocking way possible. Much of our behaviour and experience is risky and charged in an overtly sexual way.

Denying crisis character position

If, as a yearning crisis character, we are in a constant state of charge and excitement and fear, as a denying character, by contrast, we have closed down to life's stimuli, as it felt just *too* exhausting and dangerous. We are likely to be motivated by keeping excitement at bay, so it does not become 'too much' and so we do not become 'too much' for others, a very common fear we have in relating to others as a denying crisis character. As a result, we are likely to have an interesting relationship with play; limiting the amount of play and excitement we allow ourselves to experience, compared to a creative crisis character.

We are prone to experiencing ourselves as passive victims at the hands of the actions of others. At some point in our lives, this may well have been the case. Perhaps we were genuinely a passive victim at an age when we had no means to defend ourselves and feel safe enough. We tend to experience excitement as if it were outside of ourselves, rather than in our embodied experience. We deny the sexual dimension of our lives and feel awkward talking about it, yet people still find us sexually attractive, which we find extremely challenging. To counteract this, we may aim to appear androgynous, somewhat invisible and out of reach in our strategies.

Creative crisis character position
As a creative crisis character we will be well versed in knowing how to have fun with, bend, and break social rules, knowing that life is a game to be played and to be enjoyed. We can choose confidently how intimate to be with others, and have the where-withal to take responsibility for our choice and the effect those choices have on others. As a creative crisis character we know how to genuinely play (rather than to play *act*) in relationship to ourselves and others, to entertain, to pretend, to exaggerate and be wild and exciting. We can play without that play having to be overly-concerned with attractiveness or sex. We are likely to be much more at home in our own skin with our sense of attrac-tiveness and sexuality than denying and yearning crisis characters, realising that there is a choice in whether or not to engage with the sexual dimension of relating.

Reflections — reflecting on the six character positions

Having read this chapter:

- take the time and space you need to reflect on each character position in detail, sensing and feeling your way into each position
- note down and reflect upon the particular aspects of the character position(s) which are most immediately recognisable in your experience. How and when do you most notice these particular aspects of character positions? Do you resonate with the yearning, denying and/or creative aspects?
- notice with which of the character strategies and patterns you resonate, during meditation, as well as in everyday life
- reflect on how you might resonate with two or more of the character positions, and how they work in relationship with each other. For example, if you resonate with the holding character in often feeling stuck, this stuckness may hold you back in relating to others fully, which relates to your boundary character patterning and its related fear around contact and existence
- reflect on particular life themes with which you are familiar in your process and how these might link to the character position(s). You will have a chance to reflect on these more fully in the following chapter.

Chapter 7

The here and now, informed by the there and then

Having explored the six character positions in some depth, this chapter gives you the opportunity to explore and reflect upon your life conditioning so far. The purpose of this chapter is to help you to assimilate what you have learnt about the six character positions in the light of your own life events. This chapter is structured slightly differently to the last, with questions and reflections interspersed throughout the text. This chapter is an exploration of the different stages and dimensions of your life so far and a chance for you to make sense of character positions in your own experience, and at your own pace.

Through this exploration you come to understand more fully the conditions that brought you to this moment and your strategies and armouring. The point of this exploration is to illuminate and to cultivate greater awareness of yourself and others. Looking in depth at your life conditioning can be a strong and challenging process so during this time I recommend that you continue to practise loving- kindness meditation frequently, as well as other practices which you find supportive.

Even if you feel that you have already looked at and reflected upon your conditioning, give yourself the chance to engage with each section. It can be tempting to fall into the trap of thinking you have done the work you need to do for the time being, when, in fact, there may be nothing and everything to do. This work isn't about looking for problems; it's also a chance to notice what's gone well. The content here is not exhaustive and different parts will be more or less relevant to you individually. Feel free to focus on particular areas and dimensions which are particularly resonant and relevant.

Your arrival on earth

Think about what you know about your birth and the time leading up to your birth. Were you the firstborn? The youngest? The middle child? The oldest child? The only child? The only surviving child? One of a crowd? Were you wanted? Were you smothered with love? If you were adopted what sense do you make of your arrival in the world and into your adoptive family? Do you have a sense of whether or not you were welcomed? Were there significant events around the time of your birth or early years which have lodged in your family's consciousness? Are there particular family stories around your place in the world?

Painting a broader picture, bring to mind the broader context into which you were born, including generational influences. Think of the cultural, social, religious, environmental, economic and political trends and events. What stories and memories come to mind? Perhaps you are struck by how little you know about the time of your birth?

In thinking about your arrival on earth bear in mind the exploration of the boundary character position in the previous chapter, which is very much to do with this time of your life. Perhaps revisit those existential themes about whether you feel fully arrived on earth, how you approach contact with others and your 'whole' sense of your embodiment in relation to these themes. Notice how you feel in revisiting these themes from the perspective of the boundary character position.

Reflections – sketching a genogram

On a large piece of paper sketch out your family tree, drawing upon as much information as you can. Record significant relationships, locations and events, as well as names and dates. If you know very little about your family tree, or you are adopted, or you have lost touch with your family of origin, simply record what you do know.

Are there particular turning points and watersheds? Take notice of births, deaths, accidents and significant events, myths and stories. Notice how regional or world events impacted upon your family or personal history. Notice and record what you *don't* know or what feels incomplete or shadowy.

Take time to meditate and reflect upon your completed genogram. Allow yourself time for 'just sitting' with the genogram, noticing the thoughts, feelings, memories, urges and insights arising as you do this. Particularly notice the stories that arise about your origins. In reflecting do you feel you belong on the genogram? Are you a narrator? A descendent following a long, established family line? Or a spectator?

Your earliest people and situations

Bring to mind your particular family grouping or carers. Recall your parent(s), carers, stepparents, adoptive parents, foster parents, godparents, siblings, aunts, uncles, cousins, grand-parents, extended family, neighbours and friends who were more akin to family: the everyday people forming the backdrop to your daily life.

Is this a large or small group? Sociable or private? Tight knit or in disarray? Focused upon, or estranged from, family? If you grew up in your family of origin, what was, and is your sense of your family's place in the world? Did they see themselves as belonging, successful, outsiders, rich, poor, useful, with a voice? Note anything which comes to mind and any feelings, images, memories. Track your responses to different individuals and events as you recall them.

Reflections – mapping your early life

Take time to map your early life.

Start by mapping your early family grouping or the context in which you were raised. Draw yourself in the middle of a piece of paper. Working as quickly and spontaneously as you can, draw or depict the other significant and prominent people in relationship to you, in whatever way seems helpful.

Who is close to you and who is far from you? How did you choose to depict different people: with words, pictures, colours, symbols? Are your people different shapes and sizes? How are they placed both in relationship to you and to each other? What shape is your map? What intuitive sense do you make of what you have drawn? If your family group changed dramatically during your childhood, adjust your map to show the era after that change.

Map where your family lived. If you never moved, this might be a more simple, one location diagram. If you moved twenty times, map all those moves, perhaps using words, pictures, arrows, outlines of a physical map in a way which makes sense to you. Draw any other physical features that were prominent in the places in which you grew up.

Your early family or care conditioning

Our history is encoded in our body just as the rings of a tree encode the life story of that tree, including its genetic inheritance and the atmospheric conditions that were present from year to year.
Stromsted in Johnson and Grand, 1998: 157

Continue to think about your parents or carers in your early years. What images, messages, feelings and emotions immediately come to mind? Give yourself the time and space to be surprised by what appears, inviting it to show you its meaning. What was the atmosphere like in your family or early context? What were you praised for? Criticised for? Who says what in the familial messages you hear? Did this change as you grew up? Did you rebel or conform? Do you think of your childhood as happy, sad, mixed, or perhaps you never really thought about it?

Needs and wants. How were your physical and emotional needs met as a child? Did you (and do you) often feel loved and supported by your family? Do you get the sense that you were allowed to be cared for, or were you given the message from early on that you were to 'stand on your own two feet'? Were you affected strongly by the arrival of other siblings, or other competing interests, such as your parents' work or careers? Do you get a sense that you can adequately meet your needs now? Or do you particularly seek nourishment and support? If you get a sense that need is a particularly resonant theme for you, continuing to pattern your adult life, revisit the section on the oral character position in the previous chapter.

Independent steps. Were your early experiments with independence met with delight and encouragement or restriction and control? Were you allowed to play with feeling influential as you grew? Was this play validated or squashed when you were a toddler? As an adult do you long to control things, people, and events? If the themes of validation and independence have particular resonance for you, consider rereading the section on the control character position in the previous chapter.

Rules and norms. Was your early world strictly regimented, or free and easy, in terms of rules, norms and assumptions? Were you valued for being an autonomous growing little toddler and allowed to do things in your own time and space? What was the prevailing attitude towards bodily rhythms, processes and fluids? Are you very regimented in the way you currently live your life or, conversely, do you, in your eyes 'mess up' pretty routinely? Perhaps revisit the section on the holding character position if some of these things sound familiar.

Making your mark. As you started to test those around you, experimenting with your own sense of will and determination, were you met with clear, kind boundaries, or was your wilfulness met with force? Were you punished for having a will of your own? Was your will constantly overshadowed or overpowered by that of your parents or carers? If the themes of assertion and a determinedly industrious approach to life still ring true for you now, reread the section on the thrusting character in the previous chapter.

The first puberty. As you began to take on your gendered identity in the world, were you encouraged and supported to do this in your own way, or were you given strong messages to conform to certain cultural rules? Were you rewarded for fitting with the expected image of your particular gender? Are you still? Or were you free to play with those expectations? Did you experience abusive behaviour or receive unwanted attention, leading to fear of contact? Are the themes of attraction and being wanted still of defining importance to you as an adult? If so, consider revisiting the section in the last chapter on the crisis character position.

The interface of family and cultural conditioning

Begin to think more broadly about the body of people or the society of which you were a part (or felt excluded from), from your birth until you came of age as an adult. Close your eyes for a moment and let your mind wander.

Faith and beliefs. Were certain beliefs instilled in you? Were your family religious? Actively engaged in religious practice? Atheist? Agnostic? Materialists? Or following strong political convictions? Were there strong views about what was seen as ethically right or wrong? Were these discussed openly, or taken for granted as being embedded in your family culture?

Ethnicity. What was the ethnic origin of your family? How did this influence your family's view of itself and your view of yourself? Did you feel a part of society, or on the margins of society, as a result of your ethnicity? Did you face covert or overt prejudice as you grew up? Were you aware of and proud of your roots?

Class. Did your family consider themselves to be working class, middle class or upper class? How did this impact upon your family and its views and expectations? In what way was your family class conscious? Was social mobility important?

Wealth and status. Were your parents or carers rich or poor or comfortably off? Or was this never openly discussed? What views were imparted to you about money and status? Was it important to succeed in terms of material values, or to follow your heart in life?

Gendered identity. Reflect on your experience of how it was to be a boy or girl. Or perhaps you feel as though you never quite 'fitted' either category, biologically, socially, or culturally? What was your overall experience of being embodied as a boy or girl? Have you felt at home in your gendered identity? Have you felt the discomfort and dis-ease of not feeling you belonged in your particular body? Has gender and identity been a complex area? How did you, and do you, make sense of your own experience of your gender, and the impact of the expectations, hopes, fears and agendas of family, friends and wider society, in your gendered identity? Perhaps you feel at home in your own skin as a man or woman, and gender has been a fairly straightforward aspect of being alive? How openly were gender, sex and sexuality talked about in your family of origin?

Bodies and health. What were the prevailing views towards health and well-being in your family? Was this consciously considered? Did you grow up in a 'grin and bear it' culture? Or in a family priding itself on good health and fitness? Were you cared for when you were ill or in pain? What were your personal and familial responses to bodies, nakedness, intimacy, touching, hugging, kissing, sickness and illness and how did these coincide with the prevailing culture of the time? What were the messages you received regarding these? Were these messages conveyed openly, or via that which was left unsaid?

Love and sex. What messages were you given about your body, sex, love, friends, boyfriends, girlfriends, romance, passion, attraction, beauty, the opposite sex, the same sex? What behaviour did your parents or main carers role model in these different dimensions? What were your associations with sex? Notice with kindness what emerges as you reflect. How did your parents or carers model being in all sorts of different relationships? (Parent, friend, brother, sister, work mate, lover, husband, partner etc.) Bring to mind your teenage years and be with the thoughts, feelings and images which arise. Was your transition from childhood to young adulthood painful, a relief to be becoming more independent, or an exciting mystery? Recall your early experiences of sexual feelings and falling in love. Notice whether you think of yourself as an early or later developer and what that meant in your family and cultural context. If this dimension of your experience holds particular significance revisit the section in the last chapter on the crisis character position.

Reflections – An embodied lifeline

Make time to reflect upon your own experiences of embodiment through your lifetime. Bring to mind important watersheds related to your embodiment and important 'aha' moments.

Create an embodiment lifeline, visually, in words, or, better still, with a friend. This might be a linear line, drawn on paper, or a 'map' you create using the physical space of a room. What were the key events that shaped your relationship with your body? As well as more external events, this line might include significant internal realisations.

Once you have created your lifeline, make time to meditate upon it and notice what arises. Add to it and adapt it as you wish.

Leaving home.

Bring to mind your leaving home, potentially one of the most important cusps in life and an important rite of passage. Did you plan to leave home? Did it happen to you? Think about the nature of your leaving home. Was it by choice? Or because you could not think of anything better to do? Were you excited at the thought of further study or a job or escaping home? Were you following your heart? Did your parents leave before you did? Were you doing what was sensible and approved of? Were you simply longing to be free? What were your thoughts and feelings about becoming more independent? Were you excited or terrified? Is there a part of you which is yet to leave home, even though you may have physically left years ago?

Stories of your adult life

... how can we escape from the invisible threads of our family history... from the... frequent repetitions of difficult situations? In a way, we are less free than we think we are. Yet we can regain our freedom and put an end to repetitions by understanding what happens, by grasping the threads in their context and in all their complexity. We can thus finally live 'our own' lives, and no longer the lives of our parents or grandparents...
Ancelin Schützenberger, 1998:3

Many of the stories of our adult lives are inextricably shaped by the events and experiences of our childhoods. Bring to mind events, feelings, key turning points, and important relationships so far in your adult life. Let your mind and body wander over your history for as long as you wish, allowing your awareness to be drawn to the bits which needs attention.

What have been the stories of your life: stories you have told yourself and stories which others have told to you? Has your life been about conformity or rebellion? Convention or alternatives? Feeling stuck or free? Success or failure? Following in the footsteps of a particular parent or significant role model? Being a loner or being part of a community? Have you felt you belonged or have you been a constantly seeking stranger? Has the path of your life felt smooth or staccato? Has the journey been like a roller coaster or an ocean-going liner? Have you shaped your own life, or followed the lead of others, or let events unfold? Have there been points in your life when you have really broken with tradition or past habits, and changed direction? Give yourself all the time you need to consider or reconsider these stories afresh, from where you are at this point.

Work and how you spend your time

Think about what you have spent the majority of your time doing so far in your adult life. For the majority of you who need to support yourself through earning a living, this is likely to be about paid work. Think through the nature and shape of your work so far. Perhaps reflect on how you approach work, as well as the nature of your work. Is your work a vocational calling or a means to an end? Having started to explore the six different character positions, how do the themes which you have noted throw light on your approach to work, in terms of what you expect of: yourself, others, how you work and the nature of the job itself? Perhaps the themes help you to make sense of why you have been drawn to particular jobs and careers, and not to others?

Your current well-being

Metaphors often present themselves as literal symptoms in your body.

Bosnak, 1986: 31

Now reflect upon your overall well-being in the present day. In the previous section you looked at your conditioning around your body and health. Here recall as broadly as you can your history of being a bodymind: achievements, illness, addictions, accidents, food and eating, sickness, things you survived, peak moments, pregnancy and child-birth related complications, times when you relished being a bodymind, depression, life-threatening events, abuse, stress, shocks, anxiety, trauma, the effects of war, exile, torture, the ill effects of having to leave your home place, within the same country, or across borders or continents. Notice thought, feelings, sensations. Also pay attention to whether you start to distract yourself as you recall these events and what happens.

Reflect on the well-being of your family of origin and the attitudes you identified from the section on bodies and health. Reflect on the health of your own family, if you have one. Think back to your genogram, noting any accidents or illnesses or health-related themes that seemed significant. Think of your general level of health, giving yourself the chance to reconnect with your own life history and your own thoughts, feelings and memories. Bring to mind particular areas of your embodiment which you have found challenging. Perhaps reflect on how your understanding of the six character positions might throw light on how you have approached being a body and areas of apparent challenge or sensitivity in being a body.

Reflections – key people

Sketch a lineage of people who are (or have been) significant to you. Think as broadly as you can – these people may be alive or dead, family members, friends, historical figures, contemporary figures, mythical figures, animals and other than human beings. Meditate and reflect upon your completed map and notice what arises.

Relationships

What have been the most significant relationships and connections in your life? These may be intimate lover and sexual relationships, friendships, parental relationships, siblings, teachers, extended family members and key role models. Think about the relationships which have had the most influence (positive and negative) upon you; shaping who you are today. Cast your net widely in thinking about these relational influences.

Which relationships have taught you the most? Which have been most painful? Which have helped you to realise your embodiment, perhaps in mysterious or unexpected ways? Which relationships were destructive? Which relationships do you miss? Which relationships are you glad to have experienced? In which relationships have you had the most significant influence, now or in the past? Having explored character positions, reflect on how the particular themes illuminate how you approach relationships, and the nature of the relationships you have experienced.

Family and parenting (or not)

Here you are invited to explore your experience of creating your own family. Bring to mind your decision-making regarding: whether or not you wanted to have children, your future plans to have children, you or your partner's inability to conceive, or your long process in conceiving, how you had children unexpectedly, or how you had a child or children that died. Conception obviously has huge implications for your experience of embodiment, your changing relationship with your body, identity, and your sense of potency. Take time to think through your history of experiences with regards to procreation, conceiving, not conceiving, pre-birth complications, childbearing, childrearing, losing a child and any other related scenario which is relevant here.

Note what is uppermost in your experience with regards to these dimensions, and the effect of the decisions you have made (or perhaps the decisions you did not consciously make). You might consider how your experiences of conception, child-bearing and child-rearing have changed your experience of being a body. Or how your decision not to have children has impacted upon your sense of being a gendered body, in a world where the majority of people have children. You might recollect the pain of not being able to conceive, and the effect of that upon you, your body, your relationships, your embodied, cultural and societal identity.

Perhaps bring to mind your relationship to your babies that survived and any that died, knowing that they once lived inside you, if you were their mother, or your role in their creation as their father. Or bring to mind the child or children you left behind. Perhaps you are drawn to reflecting upon your experience as a stepparent, inheriting a parental type role, and your feelings associated with that. Or think about how it has been to have chosen to adopt and bring up a child. Reflect on being a parent in light of having read about the six character positions, and how your experience as a child influenced your own experience of parenting. (Tread kindly as you reflect, remembering that there is no such thing as a perfect mother or father. Each of us arrive on earth with our own volitions and patterns, as well as being influenced by familial conditioning this particular lifetime).

Now

The intention of this chapter has been to encourage you to look at the very broad canvas of your life, your conditioning and the effect of this in the past and present. Perhaps you have identified areas where you want to create the conditions to heal particular aspects of your experience, or understand certain life threads with greater clarity, gentleness, sensitivity, or compassion. You might have named patterns and events which seem significant. Being in touch with these will be useful in the next chapter, as you go on to look at how themes from character positions can support you in engaging more fully in meditation.

Having looked at your history, and in the spirit of 'starting from where you are', reorient yourself to the present day and your current experience of life. You might want to do this in a very practical way, focusing on the everyday rhythms and structures of your life and whether they support effective conditions for meditation. You might want to do this more intuitively, getting a felt sense of what needs to happen, or arise, for you to create the conditions to go deeper in meditation. It might be useful to revisit your reflections from the ends of Chapters 2 and 3, when you reviewed your experiences of meditation so far.

Remember the instruction from Yeshe Tsogyal: "Again and yet again work on whatever estranges you from meditation." (Tsogyal 2008: 689) Notice your particular stumbling blocks, and old, limiting views – some of which may need a little kind cajoling at the roots. Also notice the gateways in your experience which give you the chance to go deeper in meditation. These might consist of approaching meditation in a different way, spending more time doing a specific practice, or experimenting with how you 'work' in meditation. In dwelling on these consider inviting the 'mirror-like' wisdom of the great blue Buddha of the East, Akshobya. Simply see what is there in your experience, without adding on or discounting. Be as honest and as compassionate as you can in seeing your life, as it is, your embodiment and your meditation process, as it is, without diminishing or amplifying.

Reflections – A mosaic of your life

Now that you have reflected upon the multi-faceted nature of your life so far you might consider drawing together the threads you have encountered in the process, in honouring your life and celebrating your time on earth.

Consider bringing together all these dimensions in a kind of mosaic, collage or mandala of your life, particularly if you have creative or visual leanings (or want to develop that imaginative/visual faculty more fully, a useful aid to meditation). Try this in whatever way makes sense to you perhaps using images, photos, different media, notes and memorabilia.

Chapter 8

Meditating with character

We're not looking for causes here; we're looking for systems and consistencies. It's not a question of which one is true. It's a question of how much I can learn from each (character position).

Kurtz, 1990: 42 (author's brackets added)

Having surveyed the landscape of your relationship with meditation, your relationship with embodiment and an exploration of character positions, this final chapter focuses upon how exploring character can offer you a deeper engagement with meditation. A reminder again that character positions are neither meant to be prescriptive, or somehow linear and 'set in stone'.

Introducing character positions in the context of meditation practice is an experiment in inviting you to see what resonates with your experience. It also gives you the opportunity to see how character dynamics and strategies throw light on how you can practice more fully in and through meditation. You might build on the creative aspects of particular character positions which you can see already have a positive influence on your practice. Perhaps you will start to see with greater clarity the constraining aspects of character, such as out-dated views about yourself, and armouring in particular regions of your body.

In this chapter each character position is explored through four common themes:

- **Turning towards meditation.** This section looks at how and why you might originally have been drawn to meditation and your (likely) early responses as conditioned by the relevant character position. It also looks briefly at the meditation context you might find most conducive to meditation.

- **The benefits of meditation.** This part explores how meditation can be of benefit, bearing in mind the particular themes of each of the character positions.
- **Working edges.** These are the aspects of meditating which you find challenging and stretching, in terms of your character patterning. In engaging with the particular working edges of each relevant character position, you will unearth the most 'gold' in terms of knowing how to work in your meditation practice. Working edges are not simply challenging or difficult areas; they are also the pathways into insightful and deepening practice and 'spiritual' understanding.
- **Reflections and meditation exercises.** Each subsection ends with suggested meditation and reflections to help you to engage more fully with the themes of the particular character position and the relevant body segment.

The boundary character position

Turning towards meditation

As a boundary character we might be drawn to meditation with the aim of feeling more present and grounded. We might also be looking for a way to live less 'in our heads' and less dominated by our thoughts and analysis. Having said that, there is sometimes a popular misconception that meditation is a detached, disconnected activity in which we somehow empty our minds. In light of this depiction of meditation, it is possible that this may have been an initial attraction to us as a boundary character, given the key boundary strategy of staying detached, and 'safely' out of contact.

Until we start to meditate it is possible that we have been unaware of how much of our life we spend living in our heads. Our modus operandi is to engage and connect through our eyes;

looking and anchoring through vision, seeing, and being seen, rather than physical grounding through our feet being firmly planted on the earth (unless we are also patterned by the holding character position). For this reason, it can at first be daunting for us to close our eyes in meditation. This is particularly true when we are sitting in a crowded meditation room. Not only are our eyes shut – shutting off our primary way of locating ourselves in the world – but we are surrounded by others which can stir our other key life theme of fear of contact with others. On the other hand, we might experience a sense of relief in closing our eyes and having a rest from having to make sense of making contact with others and deciphering the multiple channels of information coming our way.

In meditating we might start to feel more present and grounded the more we become aware of the fact that we are a being with a mind *and* a body. As this sense of embodiment increases we will perhaps begin to acknowledge and face our deep-seated existential fears. Our initial work in embodied meditation is to learn to arrive, to start to feel the possibility of being more at home in our own bodies, and to be with our existential fears around contact. From a creative viewpoint, meditation will affirm our ability to access other realms and dimensions. This can be both resourcing *and* confusing, in terms of knowing which realms we actually inhabit at any one time. As we become more accustomed to our meditation process we face ever more subtle distractions in 'losing ourselves' in other realms, as well as in deep thought, analysis and reflection, running the risk of losing touch with our purpose in meditating.

Some of us shaped by boundary strategies will have taught ourselves meditation from a book. Coming to a class, and sitting with others, can feel pretty threatening if you are patterned by this character. As a way of staying safe our initial approach to meditation may be overly-logical, analytical, and perhaps mechanical and emotionally 'cool'. We may focus rather literally on the stages, rather than focusing upon our feelings and sensations in response to the stages, given that we have a tendency to be cut off from our warmer, sensual, embodied experience.

Arriving fully on our meditation cushion is an important foundation for practice. It is important for the boundary character to feel as physically comfortable as possible. Of course, this is true for all characters, but particularly the case for a boundary character, as the process of fully inhabiting our bodies, or even fully realising we are a body with a mind is a working edge. Given our boundary defence strategy of 'floating off', grounding ourselves is likely to be a long-term, or even a lifelong practice in itself.

Becoming skilled in grounding ourselves will also be helpful as an antidote to the amount of time we spend 'in our heads' (particularly if we are shaped by boundary *and* oral patterns). Early on in meditation our awareness of felt senses may be minimal. We may consider felt senses to be something of a distraction or a hindrance to meditation. In becoming more aware of our embodiment we are also likely to get a clearer sense of the everyday tensions and aches and pains in our bodies. This may be an unnerving and a somewhat new experience, and thus another dimension of our meditation process to sit with and assimilate over time.

We are likely to become increasingly aware of how much tension we expend in holding ourselves together, and the effort it takes simply to exist as a body. Earlier boundary character armouring was explored in some depth, for example, the considerable amount of tension which we hold in our bodies, and the lack of unity between our bodies and minds. As we meditate, this lack of unity will become increasingly clear to us. Simply following our breath can be a useful way of bringing the focus of our energy down into our bodies, and provide a way of being with tensions. Equally, a sense of drawing energy up from the earth can be a very grounding exercise. This might provide a stronger sense of a firm base, and engage our imaginal faculty as we sense the earth providing us with a deep sense of earthy rootedness.

It is likely that we will appreciate being lead in meditations, with a clear beginning, middle and end, and clear and logical instructions for each type of meditation being taught. Clear instructions and transitions like this can be a relief and provide safety; a rest from life's ongoing, underlying fear of struggling to know where we are in relationship to ourselves and others. Having half an hour of undisturbed time with firm, held boundaries, and smooth transitions can be a relief from the fear of having to make contact and negotiate our presence and engagement in everyday situations.

As we become more adept at meditation and accustomed to different meditation practices, we may find that our natural preference is to meditate alone. Of course, it is impossible to make accurate generalisations about this, as many of us will experience the shaping and strategies of more than one character position which may well temper this preference. In meditating alone, we know that we do not have to face turning up to a public place to meditate with others. This may feel easier on one level; yet in the long run, it may be useful for us to continue meditating with others. Meditation classes and courses will hopefully provide a supportive context in which we can face fears about contact in a creative way, thereby giving ourselves repeated and reparative experiences of feeling safe enough, enabling us to go deeper in our embodied experience as we sit.

We may find it useful to do some kind of additional body work or body movement alongside our meditation practice. This can be supportive in moving the energy and focus of attention from our heads and thoughts further down our bodies, offering the opportunity for more grounded connectedness, wider energy flow and the healing of splits in our embodiment. This can also support us to feel more present, more aware of the energy in the lower half of our bodies, and consequently less preoccupied with mental activity. With this in mind, I am reminded of a friend's comment:

> It's so liberating to finally realise, through dancing, moving and body awareness in meditation, that this sense of disconnection is not who I really am! Body-based 'stuff' is the key to getting out of my box!

The benefits of meditation

Meditation gives us the chance to assimilate our experience through stopping and being more fully present, as for my boundary friend:

> I feel much more peace in the moment, knowing there's nowhere to go, no need to make contact with others, just to be, quiet and inward.

This is important if we resonate with the boundary character position, in that our everyday strategies are 'floating off', overanalysing or dreaming. Meditating provides us – potentially, at least – with a welcome relief from the effort it takes us to make contact with others in everyday life. This will be a very significant benefit of meditation for those of us patterned by the boundary character position.

As a boundary character we have seen how we might range from being an academic through to being attuned to the mystical. Meditation offers us the opportunity to experiment with, and further develop, the multitude of channels upon which we call in processing information and engaging with different practices.

It can be a relief for us to discover a process and system of practice which can make the most of our minds, whilst encouraging a stronger sense of embodiment and grounded contact with the earth. As a boundary character we have the capacity for big visions for self, other and world in our practice, which is likely to extend beyond meditation. Given the familiarity of our struggle with being present, and what it means to be alive and making contact, we will be familiar with reflecting on existential issues, providing a useful gateway into 'spiritual' practice.

Finally, those of us with boundary character patterning are likely to realise the benefits both on and off the cushion, linked to our key life themes. A friend of mine reminded me of this, as she referred to the effect of body awareness meditation in the course of everyday life:

> I often feel disconnected from people. Now I can come back to my experience in my body when I feel disconnected from others, helping me to stay open. I never used to see the point in coming back to my body like that, and I didn't feel connected with my physical experience. Now it's so important to me.

Working edges

In learning to meditate we will start to face our views about our body: whether we have ignored our body, seen it as a nuisance, or paid it minimal attention. The process of being more aware of being a body may seem a little alien at first, and then a little painful as we realise the extent of our disconnection from self and other. Practising loving-kindness meditations are a useful foundation practice for this reason. We may find it hard to become grounded – and stay grounded – in meditation, having a stronger faculty for being in touch with the vast blue sky than the more solid, brown, earth. We might find it useful to reflect upon, and learn 'skying':

> The capacity to be in contact with those cosmic, visionary energies which we access through the crown of our heads, as well as with the earth energies we access through our feet or sacrum.
> Totton, 2003: 69

Our work is likely to be in contacting, and drawing from earth energies (unless we are also patterned by the holding character). When we are in tune with this dance between earth and sky we are less likely to lose touch with the material world and reality, approaching meditation in a less analytical and dry way. It is also useful to be aware that we might be tempted to use meditation as another strategy for 'floating off'. Meditation is not about 'floating off' (at least, not the sort of meditation I have in mind in this book), although this can be a near enemy. In meditating with a fuller, more fluid sense of our embodiment there is less chance that we will stand outside of ourselves in meditation – as a potentially alienated observer and commentator – and more chance we can invite greater awareness of our embodied feelings and emotions.

The boundary connection with the rich resourcefulness of mind and vision can be a blessing *and* a distraction. Providing we remain sufficiently grounded, the potential capacity of our boundary-conditioned mind for making connections, links, and for insightful reflection in meditation is phenomenal. Sometimes we may fear losing ourselves in meditation as we get in touch with a tangible sense of the transitory, ever-changing phenomenological nature of existence. We are no stranger to dwelling with the 'big' questions in life. Staying grounded is vital in staying with our embodied experience, and to lessen the influences of the near enemy of alienated awareness.

We may find it relatively easy to get concentrated, but this may initially be from the neck upwards, not necessarily supporting the integration of our energies. Alienated awareness can have a seriously disintegrating effect, hence the importance of balancing the energies of our heads, hearts and guts through loving-kindness, breathing meditation, mindfulness and just sitting, inviting deeper contact with each dimension of our energetic experience.

Another challenge we may face is that we may be reluctant to share much about our meditation experiences, seeing these experiences as part of our private, internal world. It is a shame if we let this fear stop us from sharing our experiences in the long-term, as they are likely to be vivid and insightful. Over time this fear is likely to subside as we form bonds with trusted friends who meditate. Developing these links can be extremely repar-ative in supporting us to make fuller and richer contact with others.

We are likely to start to feel more complete and whole as a result of meditating – fully arrived and safe from shock. This is significant and transformative boundary work, in terms of work our bodies need to complete. Developing a meditation practice can offer positive conditions for us to do this work as a boundary character. This is likely to be realised through learning to meditate with others in a safe and supportive environment, complemented by meditating at home and applying what we learn on the cushion to the rest of our lives.

Working to deepen our sense of embodiment is useful in providing us with the awareness to notice both tensions and well-being, thereby inviting the beginning of a loosening and dissolving of the armouring in our joints and muscles. It can also be very freeing for us to pay particular attention to relaxing our face, eyes, brows and cheeks in meditation, and allowing our scalp to be softer.

In thinking of work the boundary character needs to complete, I am reminded of the words of a friend, fellow meditator, and therapist, who has made tremendous changes with her relationship to her embodiment:

Through my life I've felt very ambivalent towards my body... physically I did everything slightly 'wrong' or awkwardly, not well or happily embodied. Over the years I've found a sense of fluidity and flexibility. This is quite a transformation. I feel like I'm living much more in my body. It used to be a nuisance, it needed feeding, etc etc and I lived my life in my mind. Now I have a much kinder, accepting care towards my body...

Reflections and meditation exercises

Note down thoughts, feelings, memories and images that rang true as you read this chapter. In thinking about what you have read, reflect on the following pairs and notice your embodied responses:

welcome/unwelcome, numb/acute, safe/unsafe, dead/alive, creative/destructive, inner/outer, scattered/gathered, disappear/present, self/other, hot/cold, fragile/strong.

Meditation exploring your head:

Take time to meditate and reflect on these themes. Start with a general body awareness (see the reflections section of Chapter 3) and then move your focus to your head.

Begin by noticing the shape and form of your head from the outside. Feel the weight of your head, poised on your shoulders. Allow your head to find a resting place by gently tilting it forward and back and from side to side. Imagine a sense of melting of your scalp, allowing tensions to soften from the top of your head in a downwards motion. Allow your jaw to join in with this softening motion. Notice the muscles in your face and cheeks getting heavier. Pay attention to your eyes. Close your eyes. Let your eyes relax: not having to see, look, and gauge the looks of others, if only for a few moments. Feel the droopiness of the muscles around your eyes as you do this. Sense the effort it takes to keep your eyes working so hard. Notice the movements of your head: your breath, what you hear, and the connection of your head with other parts of your body.

Explore your head from the inside. Notice the air moving through your head as you breathe. Sense the moisture in your mouth, nose, eyes and ears. Feel the heat of your head and the different temperature at various points. Be aware of the cavities and spaces in your head: your ears, nose, the back of your throat and right inside your head. Notice areas of tension and areas of well-being as you pay attention. Notice your thoughts and feelings as you focus.

Grounding and skying meditation:
Start with a body awareness meditation, taking as long as you wish to feel really grounded and present. Begin by noticing your energy throughout your body. Then gradually move the focus of your attention to the flow of your energies between the sky and earth. Now bring a kindly attention to energy in and around your head, neck and shoulders. Imagine that the different parts of your body are connected by an invisible thread. The thread stretches from the earth all the way up through your spine, running up the centre of your body, towards the sky. Notice how your embodied experience is contained by your skin, marking the boundary between inner and outer. Take some time to explore how it feels to be held in this skin. Notice whether your energy extends beyond your skin. How far does it extend?

Broaden your awareness so you notice your bottom on the chair or cushion. Feel the contact of your legs, feet and toes with the earth. Feel as heavy as you can, allowing your weight and energy to sink into the earth, allowing it to take your weight. Breathe your energy downwards, into your belly, genitalia, thighs, lower legs, feet and toes. Imagine feeling really rooted like a tree with huge roots, soundly anchored to the earth.

Take as much time as you wish in experimenting with moving your awareness between your top and your tail; sky and earth. Notice the different sensations of energy and channels of information as your awareness expands.

The oral character position
Turning towards meditation
There are a multitude of reasons why those of us patterned by the oral character position are drawn to meditation. Perhaps we have found meditation useful as a way of shedding light on the nagging sense of need in our everyday experience. Or perhaps we are seeking more supportive and nurturing conditions, wishing to build our inner resources through establishing a meditation practice. We might want to find a way to make sense of suffering and its origin. Perhaps we are motivated by under-standing our disappointments and our sense of deflation with ourselves, others and life, learning how to manage the resulting anxiety through becoming more rested and grounded.

In contrast to the boundary character, as an oral character we are likely to find it easier to learn meditation in a class or course context, appreciating the support of that environment in which we can connect with others. The exception to this is if we are patterned by the denying oral character position. Those of us with this patterning may prefer learning meditation at home. We might do this for years before venturing to a meditation class, feeling that we are better off relying on ourselves than others.

In setting up the initial conditions for meditation, it is useful to make sure we have everything we feel we need to support our practice. I recall a friend who is influenced by this character position. I can picture her in our local meditation room with her bottle of water, tissues, blankets and her bag of useful things. It is indeed helpful to know what supports us in settling in meditation, particularly early on in setting up our practice. It is also helpful to keep an eye on what we feel we need in order to meditate, so it does not become a bit of an obsession. It can be helpful to remember that our habits change over time.

In starting to meditate it will be important for us to feel grounded, bringing our energy, focus and attention lower in our bodies. It might be particularly useful to begin meditating with body awareness, starting from our head and moving our focus of awareness and energy downwards, feeling the earth beneath our bottoms, legs and feet. Those of us with this patterning tend towards being ungrounded, so working with this will be important in setting up effective conditions in meditation; really feeling a firm base of support.

Of all the character positions, those of us with oral character conditioning are likely to experience most acutely the themes of lack, inner emptiness, suffering, and the injustice of everyday life. Remember the links between the oral character and depression explored earlier. If we are interested in Buddhism as well as practising meditation, this can be a very useful (if deeply uncomfortable) insight in understanding the nature of 'dukkha' – the unsatisfactory nature of life which arises in dependence upon craving and grasping for things, people, sensations and so on.

Craving is seen as one of the three 'poisons' in traditional Buddhist terms, the others being hatred and delusion. Experiencing inner lack and need will be strikingly familiar territory for the oral character. This is likely to have lead us on an endless search for support in relationships, friendships, jobs and so on. Sitting with this sense of inner lack can be uncomfortable and profoundly transformational for the oral character. I am reminded of the words of a friend, conditioned by both the oral and crisis character positions:

meditation is a refuge during states of misery and grief, it can transform me.

145

The benefits of meditation

The immediate benefit of meditation for those of us with oral character patterning is the chance to stop and pay attention to our internally-oriented experience, rather than the constant outward search for things and people which we perceive will fulfil our needs. This potential benefit is likely – at times – to be experienced as a discomfort, particularly in sitting with that grating inner lack and sense of need. In the longer-term it will become easier, or at least more familiar, to find internal supports in meeting our own needs, distinguishing between needs and wants and seeing how habitually our relating to others is coloured by our perceived needs.

Earlier I said that learning to meditate in the context of a meditation class is likely to be beneficial for the oral character. This context might offer a way of working with the life themes of neediness through interactions with fellow meditators. As an oral character, practising meditation in the company of friends and meditators can be helpful in at least two ways. Firstly, as a form of practical support and encouragement, and secondly, as a way of realising that life's suffering is universal and not unique to our experience. Everyone can benefit from reflecting on the universality of suffering (the first of the 'four noble truths' in Buddhism) and as oral characters we will be very familiar with a tangible sense of our own suffering. It is also likely that we will find it easier to be in touch with, and perhaps more vocal about, injustice. Getting to know a fellow meditator and hearing how they find meditation can provide mutual support as we learn about need in relationship, both on and off the cushion, with ourselves and others.

If we have become interested in Buddhism as well as meditation, we are likely to be drawn to the big picture and the challenge of practising the Dharma – the teachings of the Buddha and the path of practice. In resonating with the recognition of suffering and the often unsatisfactory nature of everyday life, we are likely to become interested in the causes of suffering. This can be a real inspiration to us and we might find we express ourselves strongly: voicing our own suffering, through to fighting injustices and championing important causes on behalf of others.

Oral character patterning focuses on the mouth and jaw, so anything to do with expression and all oral activities (eating, sucking, drinking, talking, biting, chewing, singing, kissing) are highlighted. With this in mind, we might find that we are drawn to mantra recitation; an integrating and grounding devotional Buddhist practice; and other forms of vocalised ritual. Or, conversely, we mind find it difficult to enter into relationship with such vocal practice. Whichever way this tendency goes, this is likely to hold stronger associations and resonances for the oral character than for the other character positions.

For the denying oral character meditation is likely to be beneficial in providing the conditions conducive to the loosening of the self-view and armouring which tells the story of never needing anyone. Meditation may offer us the conditions to contact a real sense of our own needs, perhaps for the first time. This is likely to be deeply unsettling. It might mean that we get into a 'push and pull' struggle (consciously or subconsciously) in mediating between our engrained sense of 'going it alone', and our growing realisation of interconnection. Perhaps we will practise at home alone for phases, whilst this pattern works itself out.

The other benefit of meditation for the oral character is that we are likely to be very interested in different meditation techniques. Oral character patterning gives us a strong appetite for life and learning, extending to meditation and practice. This is likely to be fuelled by our changing sense of ourselves as a result of meditation. We are likely to feel liberated, and freer of the suffering which comes from being disappointed by life (and people) not meeting our needs. Our excitement in communicating this to others around us is likely to rise to the fore. This enthusiasm, particularly during a bright and enthusiastic phase, can be very fruitful and can lead us into other areas of practice. For example, we might be inspired by the aspect of the bodhisattva ideal which relates to the liberation from suffering and injustice of all sentient beings.

Working edges

The conservation and transformation of energy is what gets me on my meditation cushion, working with my deep-seated samskaras (volitional habits) that I'm deeply fatigued. My pattern is burn bright, go dark. When the energy goes, I fall into grief.

The working edge which may quickly become apparent is our very oral disappointment that meditation is not a 'cure all' for suffering. Like my friend above, as an oral character we are particularly susceptible to highs and lows or burning bright and going dark, in terms of the phases of our mood. Meditation is a process which takes, time, energy, commitment, calling upon our faith and confidence in ourselves, our practice and our capacity to face life head-on (with compassion). No one else can do it for us – only we can put in the hours on the meditation cushion.

I am reminded of a comment from Vessantara, a friend and Buddhist teacher. A central act of Buddhism is "going for refuge to the three jewels." This describes the process of orienting our lives and practice around the three 'jewels': namely the Buddha, Dharma and Sangha. The Buddha is the founder of Buddhism (the historical figure Siddhartha Gautama), the Dharma refers to the teachings of the Buddha, and the Sangha is the spiritual community. Vessantara points out that there is a fourth jewel: ourselves. To practise effectively and go for refuge, we need "a certain basic faith" in our own potential as a human being in going for refuge (Vessantara, 1994: 87).

This 'fourth jewel' teaching is a valuable reminder for all of us. For the oral character position, valuing ourselves as the fourth jewel will be about appreciating our particular qualities and understanding our dynamics around need, gradually seeing our patterning of either tending to look outside of ourselves for support or, alternatively, only looking inwards for support (the denying oral character position).

Meditation practice acts as a powerful mirror, highlighting our habits, preferences, tendencies and shining light on our blind spots. For those of us with oral patterning, our deep sense of inner need will be mirrored back. We will see ever more clearly the transactional nature of our relationships with others, and the discrepancy between what we feel we need and what we actually get. Many of us bargain with reality, and the oral character version of this will be around support from others versus relying upon our own resources. Through going deeper in our process in and around meditation, it is likely that our sense of disappointment and frustration will ease, or at least we will understand this dynamic more fully, gradually softening our views and expectations.

We may find that we are drawn into a cycle with meditation – rather like the oral strategies towards life. When we are feeling more energised and inspired we feel very drawn to, and inspired by, meditation. When this phase comes to an end, and our inner balloon bursts, our meditation will be impacted. During a 'burst balloon' phase we may have a tendency to avoid meditation, as it feels too painful and challenging. Great fruits can come from sitting with this in meditation, inviting loving-kindness into our experiences of our inner lack (or any other painful emotions) in gently refilling our inner balloon.

Whilst 'sitting with' brings fruit, it can also be scary. Staying with pain and feelings of isolation can be daunting. I am mindful here of not confusing character patterned feelings of inner lack with a more profound sense of a heightened awareness of the continual flow of events and the emptiness of all things, in terms of nothing having a fixed, substantial identity. One woman friend, patterned by the oral and control characters, captured beautifully the moment during meditation, when she contacted the yawning sense of emptiness inside herself and how this became an important metaphor for her subsequent practice:

When I first meditated, I remember having a sense of levitating above myself and above the rupa (the Buddha statue) on the shrine. I saw myself as the rupa. I was just the brass and I was empty. I was a great big, lonely shell with nothing inside. I needed to grow an interior landscape. This has been my task; to grow a landscape. (Author's brackets added).

Growing an inner 'landscape' is an apt way of describing oral work. That work might include learning to manage our relationship with need, providing the conditions for greater balance between 'burn bright' and 'going dark' cycles, and staying sufficiently grounded to carry on sitting in meditation. Relationships can help with this inner landscaping work, providing support and encouraging us to see that we can dare to rely upon our resources. Once our honeymoon phase with meditation is over, we are more likely to show our sulkier and more cutting aspects in relating to others. The cutting nature of our speech is likely to emerge when we realise we are alone in meditation: no one can support us during sessions, apart from ourselves.

Each of us react differently to stress, including the stress which arises during meditation: as a boundary character we are likely to disappear into our heads and complex thoughts; as an oral character we are likely to become anxious, self-pitying and critical; as a control character we are likely to long to take charge with even greater gusto; as a holding character we are likely to turn inwards with a sense of shame; as a thrusting character we look to the next opportunity to put others down and boast of our own achievements; and as a crisis character we will want to entertain and create drama in diverting real contact. There is no shame in seeing our very human resistances. The trick is to create more space and awareness around our resistances, so we feel freer in choosing how to respond, gradually transforming the energy of those resistances.

Patterned by the oral character, we are likely to find it supportive to have a chance to share our meditation and practice with others. This might take the form of going on retreat, having meditation interviews and, more informally, being part of a network or community of meditators. The other dimension which we may find supportive is learning how and why meditation works. Because of our love of communicating and sharing ideas being part of a study group is likely to be very useful in providing a supportive context.

Understanding how meditation 'works' (and when and how it doesn't work!) can build confidence and trust, helping to plant up our inner landscape. Whereas as a holding character we might feel inhibited in talking about inspirations and challenges in meditation – through fear of being criticised – as an oral character we are likely to enjoy the experience of articulating and sharing ideas.

With regards to this dimension of studying and practising with other meditators, our relationship with our meditation teachers is likely to be significant in working with the life theme of need and support. Ideally, our teacher will offer a balance of reassurance and challenge, rather than tipping towards one pole or another. As we have seen, the lone nature of meditation will sometimes be a challenge to those of us patterned by the oral character. The support of a kindly and experienced teacher can be invaluable in encouraging us to stay with our process, keep going (especially through low phases), cultivating confidence and faith in our meditation process, without getting into a rescuing relationship.

Reflections and meditation exercises

Make a note of things with which you resonated as you read this chapter. Begin by reflecting on the following pairs, noticing your embodied responses:

Hungry/satiated, self/other, empty/full, low/high, justice/unfairness, brightness/darkness, abundance/lack, laugh/cry.

Meditation exploring your jaw, mouth, neck:

In this meditation, you are invited to begin with a general body awareness and then focus upon the area around your jaw, mouth and neck.

Before you begin make sure you have everything you need in sitting to meditate. Commit yourself to a certain time period of meditation and recollect your purpose. In preparing for meditation you might chant a mantra, if that is a practice with which you are familiar, integrating the energies of your head, heart and gut.

Begin by noticing the shape and form of your mouth, jaw and cheeks externally. Feel the sensations in your jaw, reflecting on all the things you do with this area of your body and making those movements in a slightly exaggerated way, e.g. sucking, licking, swallowing, biting etc. Invite a sense of relaxation in your jaw, softening any tensions and where possible, allowing it to relax. Let your lips relax and mouth droop. Imagine a softening through the whole lower half of your head, allowing tensions to dissolve as they drain away down your neck and eventually down into the earth. Notice the muscles in your jaw and mouth getting heavier, noticing really subtle sensations and softening. Scan the rest of your head, to invite a softening of any other tensions. Notice the tiny, almost undetectable movements of your mouth, jaw, neck.

Explore your mouth and jaw internally. Begin by noticing the air moving through your mouth as you breathe. Come back to the breath as an anchor, as and when you become distracted or fearful. Use the breath to deepen your experience of each area of your jaw and mouth. Notice the sensations: listen to any noises and feel the air on your top lip. Sense the spaces in your mouth and jaw and pay attention to these as you breathe. Visualise or sense the overall area your jaw occupies in your head.

Notice your mouth. Sense the moisture in your mouth. Get a sense of the hardness of your teeth, compared to the soft moisture of your gums. Spend several minutes noticing the different elements in your jaw: the heavy earth element of the bones, the moistness of your spit, the heat and temperature of your jaw, the air and spaces in your mouth, and your awareness itself as you focus on this part of your body. Take time to soften and relax as you scan your jaw and mouth, relaxing even the tiniest of muscles. Notice any responses from this area as you pay it kindly, mindful, attention.

Once you have sensed your way into the different parts of your jaw and mouth, broaden your awareness to include your whole embodied experience. Gently bring the meditation to an end.

The control character position

I don't like being out of control. As soon as I feel out of control, I get agitated (places her hand on her heart). I know I'm losing control, then fear sets in, because I don't like being in that place. Since practising – because of mindfulness – I can see when I get agitated. I can see this person who's gone out of control, I can see what they're doing and thinking, yet I can't stop. But what I desperately want to do is to get back into my body and say "stop this controlling!" And *that* is my practice. Meditation interview with a friend (author's brackets and italics added)

Turning towards meditation

It is interesting to reflect on how those of us with control character strategies and armouring were drawn to meditation in the first place. Perhaps we wished to learn meditation in order to become more effective in our working lives. Or perhaps we reached a point of burnout in our work and were looking for new strategies for relaxation and work-life balance. We might have been drawn to meditation having heard a particularly charismatic meditation teacher.

In everyday life we are more inclined to shape events and people around us, rather than turning inwards to be with ourselves and our experience. In the early stages of meditating it may feel, at best, a little alien, and at worse, pretty frightening, in that we may feel small and insignificant. Inwardly, we find it very challenging to be with our sense of vulnerability (let alone show any vulnerability), so sitting in meditation and running the risk of facing ourselves more fully might not be our obvious activity of choice.

I recall asking a friend with this patterning about her early meditation experiences. She recounted her response when the meditation teacher suggested that people close their eyes: "You are joking!? There are all these people sitting behind me and to the side of me!" She laughed at herself and said she did not know quite what she thought they might do to her, but she didn't want to close her eyes in a roomful of complete strangers. This sense of having to know what is going on and wanting to be in charge is a strong theme for those of us who resonate with the control character position.

Once we reach the meditation cushion there may be a sense of relief in having timeout from being a constant mover and shaker. I remember the same friend saying that during meditation she finds it a huge relief to realise that she's not actually the centre of the universe! It may take time to really realise and appreciate this. Once we have acclimatised, realising that there is no one and no events to shape during meditation, we will probably find that our desire to control things extends to managing and shaping our meditation practice and experience. We might be overly focused in following the instructions, or the particular object of concentration in the meditation, rather than tuning inwards towards our experience. Like all habits to which we bring awareness, this will change over time, as we become more aware of what is going on and our particular approach and hindrances.

We are likely to find it effective to get in touch with our purpose in a very live and engaged way in meditation, as explored in Chapter 2. It will make sense to us to do this, given that we tend to be very purposeful. We might also pay particular attention to our heart and chest areas, allowing this to be as spacious and as open as possible as we sit to meditate. One of the exercises at the end of this section looks at how we might approach this.

The benefits of meditation

The main benefit of meditating is giving ourselves the chance to stop and just be: providing a much-needed rest from having to be in a role and position of control. Our strong desire to shape and plan – which can be fantastic qualities – are a double-edged sword in meditation, and it will take time, as it does with any character patterning, to become fully aware of the helpful and less helpful aspects of these internal dynamics. Giving ourselves the chance to just *be* provides the open space for us to meet ourselves more fully, understanding with loving-kindness and mindfulness what motivates us. This brings us more fully in touch with our hearts, and the heart of our being, which will in turn free energy, making more energy available to us during meditation.

In going deeper in meditation, we are likely to become increasingly aware of our self-views. It will soon become apparent that our desire to shape and plans things is inextricably linked to our view of ourselves as a valid and useful human being. Over time, the conditions provided in meditation support us to see that we are a valid human being purely because we are alive, breathing and unique, rather than as a result of our life strategies of controlling the world and its beings.

In terms of the benefits of particular meditation practices, we may find loving-kindness practices extremely reparative. This practice gives us the chance to actively transform our intentions towards ourselves and others. Given that we have some expertise in understanding how to get others to do what we want them to do, we may find this practice particularly engaging in looking more closely at our intention.

The other way in which it is likely to be very beneficial is that it focuses upon both our heart and mind energies. The chest and heart area tend to be the most armoured for the control character, so the effects of engaging the heart in practice are far-reaching. The more we practice loving-kindness meditation, the more opportunities we give ourselves to realise that our longing for validation through control can be expanded and loosened in the context of cultivating and receiving universal loving-kindness for all beings, no longer limited by our narrower self-views. We will also give ourselves the chance to realise the expression of our boundless hearts: embodied exemplars of loving-kindness.

Working edges

Meditation is an opportunity to really touch how I'm *feeling* and not how I'm *facing* the world. I've learnt to put that armour aside and be really vulnerable in meditation. Sometimes I don't do that, sometimes I can't do that, some part of me is too well-defended. That's what happens.

Meditation interview with a friend.

As a control character we are accustomed to setting up our lives as though we are mistresses or masters of our universe. These dynamics and tendencies will be strongly mirrored back as we meditate. We may find this uncomfortable – as my friend in the quote above – given how we feel we need our heart armour to face the world. It can take a while to adjust and to find out for ourselves what meditation is *really* about. We might resonate with the quote above, knowing that at times we are unable to allow that sense of vulnerability in meditation by letting down our guard. The benefit of meditating, as we have seen, is that we gradually realise that we can meet ourselves fully, as we are, not just the part of us which seeks to shape, and as a result start to meet others more fully as they are.

We are likely to meet our resistances fairly early on in meditating, realising quickly that there are no people and things around to manage – simply us and our experience as a reference point. Once we have become accustomed to the form of a particular meditation practice, we may hit another layer of resistance, in not quite allowing ourselves to let go into the process of meditation, trying to control the process, staying in our metaphorical driving seat.

One advantage we are likely to have is that we do not give up easily, which really is in our favour in persisting with meditation. As we go deeper into our reflections on the control character position and how these coincide with our experience, our bodies will gradually start to do the healing work needed. What will be important is to gradually soften around our tendencies to plan and organise. As these tendencies soften, we will have more space to listen and tune into the underlying messages of our heart, a very important area of our bodies.

Some working edges we experience are influenced by where we are in our lifecycle and how that coincides with the strategies of a particular character position. I am reminded of a dear friend in his mid-seventies, patterned in part by the control character position. He finds that he contacts his own mortality strongly during meditation. Over the past ten years he says he has noticed much more acutely the ageing of his own body and his emotional response to the fact that he's in the latter phase of his life. He sits with noticing this fear of losing control in meditation (for him, echoing the fear of losing control at the time of death), and the sense of isolation from others he feels whilst he meditates, which can heighten his existential anxiety about death. Perhaps pause to think about where you are in your own lifecycle and the impact of this upon your particular responses to meditation and embodiment.

In supporting these working edges, the context in which we learn meditation is likely to be significant. Being shaped by the control character position we will need to respect the meditation teacher if we are to be receptive to learning anything from them. We may notice ourselves testing their knowledge, experience, and wisdom to make sure they know their 'stuff' well enough to teach us. We will want to know that the teacher has the skills and experience for the job, if we are to trust them and put our heart into practising. This may bring some conflict: we might want to watch our tendency to make assumptions and snap judgements, based upon our assessment of who should be doing what.

Given that we are very effective in shaping events and people, it is highly likely that we will become involved beyond simply attending a meditation class. In an indirect way, this can be really useful in helping us to set up conditions to go deeper in meditation. Feeling that we are a useful part of the organisational life of a community of practitioners – particularly through building mutually trusting relationships – we are likely to feel more at ease in the realm of meditation.

Reflections and meditation exercises

Notice what caught your attention as you read this chapter. Begin by reflecting on the following pairs, particularly noticing your heart response:

Front of stage/backstage, soft-hearted/hard-headed, being somebody/being nobody, fame/infamy, small/big, visibility/invisibility.

Meditation exploring your heart, chest and upper body:

Take time to meditate upon your whole upper body area. Begin with a general body awareness (see Chapter 3) and then pay attention to your heart, chest and upper body. Perhaps do some loving-kindness for a few minutes, bringing your awareness to your heart energies and intentions and the warm, expansive quality of loving-kindness.

Begin by noticing the shape and form of your upper body: its density, form, the effect of gravity, and the space your physical form occupies. Notice your front, back and sides. Invite a kindly internal tone as you scan these areas. Start to notice the sensations in this area – your overall energy levels and feelings of tension and well-being. Be aware of how you hold your upper torso. Perhaps push back your shoulders and then curl your shoulders inwards, exaggerating these movements to notice how different they feel. Invite a sense of relaxation, particularly in your chest. Use the breath to soften this area, breathing in as far as you can, allowing your chest to really puff up, then relaxing on the out breath and inviting a softening wave of relaxation down through your torso, making sure as much air is expelled as possible. Feel the movement of your diaphragm. Starting from your shoulders, invite the bones and muscles in your torso to relax, allowing gravity to take effect, allowing the energy in your chest area to move as it chooses.

Explore this area inwardly. As you breathe, notice the spaces inside your chest cavity, into which your air-filled lungs expand. Notice this for several breaths. Notice whether the sensations feel similar on the left-hand and right-hand sides of your body. As you breathe be aware of the rising and falling of your diaphragm, feeling the wave-like motion through your torso. Get really interested in your breath and notice where it takes you, in terms of thoughts and feelings. As you gradually let go, let your body breathe you, rather than you controlling the pace and depth of your breath.

Notice the energy around your heart: your emotional headquarters. Feel the heat of your heart, the longings of your heart, the pumping of blood and the moisture of your heart area, perhaps the heaviness of your heart, and really attend to what you hear, see, sense and notice in thoughts, feelings, movements, impulses, memories and images. Extend this awareness outwards, as you gradually bring the meditation to a close. Take the time to notice how you approach the transition from meditation to your next activity.

The holding character position
Turning towards meditation
The holding character is likely to be drawn to meditation to provide a supportive context for exploring experience, particularly those bits which feel inherently 'wrong' and 'stuck'. Those of us with this character patterning are likely to be familiar with having to work with feelings of low self-worth, shame, and guilt, which can arise from feeling that what is inside of us is somehow 'bad' or 'wrong', or 'bad' *and* 'wrong'.

On a more physical level those of us with holding character

patterning are likely to be drawn to meditation as a means of making more pliable this sense of stuckness, which we experience physically and energetically. We might wish to learn to make decisions and live more spontaneously, feeling freer in our sense of our embodiment, rather than feeling shackled and glued to the spot, unable to make a move and getting caught up in a destructive cycle of shame.

In learning meditation we will find it useful to be in a supportive meditation environment. The more spacious and safely held this is, the better. It will be particularly important for us to know the parameters of what is expected of us, in terms of the structure of the class or event, for example, which teachers will be leading the class and which meditation practice will be taught and for how long.

As a holding character we are likely to find it quite straight-forward to find ease in meditation posture, even if we are completely new to meditation. We are also likely to find it easier than some to feel grounded and earthed. For those of us with this character patterning, feeling grounded is accessible and familiar, unless we are also strongly patterned by the boundary and/or oral character positions, in which case we are likely, energeti-cally, to move between the heavens and the earth! What can be more challenging in our grounding is setting up the conditions so that this sense of grounding does not solidify into that all too familiar sense of feeling completely immobilised and fearful of impending criticism.

Those of us patterned by the holding character position may invest a sense of security in meditation, linked to this early ability to feel grounded, and at home with sitting still on the meditation cushion. This reminds me of a friend who is shaped by this character position:

I like the fact that meditation has happened over thousands of years. When I sit to meditate, I feel like I'm following that tradition. I feel a stable base; tradition is the seat I'm sitting on, which helps me feel safe.

The benefits of meditation

Meditation provides the conditions for us to start to feel more spacious and more okay about who we are as a person, standing in our own 'spiritual' potency more fully and more frequently. We are likely to realise, perhaps for the first time, the ease with which we feel grounded, which can be a resource and something which often does not come easily to other characters. It is important, however, to note that this sense of groundedness is not necessarily tantamount to feeling at home with ourselves. Meditation does provide the conditions for 'stuck' feelings to start to loosen their grip and for us to gain greater insight into our sense of shame.

The structured nature of many meditation practices can be a relief in that we will soon learn the protocol and procedure linked to particular practices. This in itself is likely to provide a strong basis of routine and safety, given that it will feel beneficial for us to be in an objective context which is timed, held, and with known procedures. As we saw earlier, this stems back from our original sense of often feeling we got it 'wrong' as a child and the resulting shame.

As we sit with ourselves in meditation, with our tendencies and views, the more we are likely to sense our autonomy as a human being and our freedom to be in situations in which we have the space and time to reach our own decisions. This is in contrast to earlier experiences, in which we felt a pressure to act, and an equally strong corresponding sense of feeling stuck, for fear of getting in wrong. The more we sit in our own time, practising at our own pace and in a held space with others, the more potent will be our energetic sense, giving ourselves the potential to go even deeper in meditation.

We have the potential to be a positive pillar of strength in the way we approach practice and the way we are in relationship to others in our 'spiritual' community. In our most creative moments we have a natural affinity for bridging the gap between the earth and the heavens. This can be a great asset in some 'spiritual' communities where there can be a danger that practice can become all about the head: air and mental activity, rather than earthed and grounded wisdom in tune with nature's cycles.

Working edges

We might experience a strong initial resistance to turning inwards and looking at what is inside us. Even engaging with a detailed body awareness meditation or following the breath may elicit resistance. We can experience a deep fear that we are 'rubbish', as we felt when we were young and punished. There can be a strong fear of turning inwards as well as a parallel fear of being 'pushed' or pressurised beyond our comfort zones and into unknown territory, where the rules and regulations are unknown, leading to a feeling of immense fear. We are likely to be fearful of being criticised by others (and our self-critic is likely to be fairly vocal and deeply felt) on account of not doing it 'right' because of our fear that we ourselves are not quite 'right'.

When we come across these sorts of resistances, our hindrance of choice is likely to be that of sloth and torpor. Traditionally, this hindrance is associated with a state where we tend to become sleepy, heavy, and slothful, finding it hard to raise the energy to meditate. Tiredness can be the result of a lack of sleep or due to hard work, but as a hindrance it is an expression of a resistance to being with our experience. It might be helpful to pay attention to our experiences of sloth and torpor, as it might parallel times when we feel particularly 'stuck' and over-grounded in our responses to everyday life situations.

Another edge might be our relationship with our meditation teacher. I purposely used the word 'pushed' in the section above, as being pushed is often the way we experience an instruction, or even a casual suggestion from a friend. A comment that can seem quite innocuous to those patterned by other character positions can be heard as a command, criticism or a pushy suggestion by a holding character. As a holding character we are, of course, not alone in being sensitive to this, but it can be a prominent feature of this particular character. This sensitivity originates from earlier life experiences when we felt forced to abide by overbearing commands or rules, bypassing our own internal regulation.

It is likely that the negative aspects of our carer's commands will be transferred to the meditation teacher at some point, consciously or unconsciously. We might get into being a 'good girl' or 'good boy' with regard to being good at meditating and following the instructions, whilst secretly resenting the teacher. If we also recognise oral character patterning in our armouring and strategies, as well as holding, the chances are that our experience of ourselves might – covertly, at least – be a bit smug, as we feel better than others at meditation. It can take years to reveal this pattern to ourselves, and to practise more autonomously, following our own internal rhythms and regulation, rather than waiting to be told by the teacher, with the ensuing, covert intrapsychic tug-of-war. This is not a problem or a weakness; it is just one of the ways in which we will learn from our deepening relationship with ourselves, our meditation practice and those around us. At first we are likely to focus upon following the meditation method. In time we can learn to follow a more intuitive felt sense and thus choose to trust and go with that feeling.

The internal and relational tug-of-war dynamic mentioned above is part of the passive-aggressive pattern emerging in relationship to meditation practice and the meditation teacher. Finding autonomy, a strengthening sense of worth, and a developing confidence in becoming more embodied is likely to be critical in relationship to meditation. Relying upon ourselves and our practice is vital, rather than relying upon the external affirmation of a teacher. In the long run the healing effect is that we are less inclined to relate to those around us as if they are our original carer, instead acting more autonomously.

In terms of the work our bodies need to complete, we are likely to become increasingly aware of our tendencies and urges to 'hold on' and 'hold in', versus a greater sense of spaciousness – even limitlessness – that can arise in meditation. This may be a difficult edge, as letting go and being in touch with more of ourselves can feel daunting. If we start to study and practise Buddhism as well as meditation, we will soon come across the teaching of how we can cause ourselves suffering through trying constantly to hold on to, and identify with our experience, rather than experiencing something and then letting it go. This teaching may resonate strongly with those of us with this conditioning. I am reminded of my friend:

> Some of the realisations I've had in meditation challenge me deeply. If I meditate and go deeper, it dawns on me more and more that I can't hold on to things, it's not going to work as a strategy. I find this threatening.

Our engrained sense of wanting to hold on – perhaps to the point of becoming stuck – will at some point be deeply challenged in meditation. This stuckness can manifest itself in self-imposed rules which can be a form of self-sabotage and a self-fulfilling prophesy in ensuring a sense of feeling worthless. For example, views like: "If I don't meditate everyday I'm a failure." Such a view can mean we blame ourselves for 'messing up' with regards to meditation. The creative holding manifestation of this is the ability and capacity to really relish our time, space, and energy to meditate. Then we can really hold our own and take our space.

We may find it easier to meditate as part of a class, given that we find lead meditations invaluable, further supporting our conditions for being with challenging dynamics. In hearing clear instructions we know what is expected of us, which can help us to get on with the practice, as well as ensuring that we know what we are supposed to be doing, thereby avoiding being criticised for getting it 'wrong'. In fact we may find a sense of relief in meditating as we realise that the teacher has no way of knowing whether or not we are getting it 'right' or 'wrong' in the moment. In this scenario what is inside us and what is going on is purely our business, which may be extremely reparative in our gathering sense of autonomy. When meditating alone we may be more likely to not quite commit to meditating, because the space is not held by another. This can easily lead to a vicious circle of self-sabotage and guilt.

We can find it difficult to make sense of meditation instruction which is unclear, too detailed, or delivered too quickly or erratically. Ideally, those of us with this conditioning need to be kindly but definitely guided and invited rather than feeling 'told', respecting our autonomy as individuals. This sort of environment respects the integrity of the learning meditator, with gentle permission and lots of time and space to assimilate and absorb.

Admitting to others that we feel stuck in relationship with ourselves or our meditation can feel embarrassing and difficult. We might find it challenging to be open and honest in meditation interviews, or even talking to friends about meditation. Another friend with strong holding patterning expressed this sense of deep-seated shame:

I feel shame in talking about meditation and saying it as it really is. I feel like it's actually not alright to feel like this.

Ideally, our meditation teachers and friends will bear in mind our need for gentle spaciousness. Our lifework is to respect our own grounded sensitivity and to be aware of how easily criticism can result in self-sabotage or a passive-aggressive dynamic, both within us, and turned upon others.

Reflections and meditation exercises

Begin by setting aside a time and space to reflect on this chapter. What caught your attention? Perhaps make a note of these. Reflect on the following pairs, noticing your embodied thoughts and feelings:

Holding/releasing, pushing/being pushed, orderliness/messiness, inside/outside, covert/overt, safe/exposed, active/passive, pride/shame.

Meditation exploring your buttocks, thighs and shoulders:

Take time to settle into meditation, beginning with a general body awareness and noticing your purpose and starting point. Feel your contact with the ground, through your feet, legs and bottom. Pay attention to your contact with the ground, your weight on the earth, and the shape of your form, poised on your chair or cushion. Soften to the sense of gravity in allowing your body to relax a little more on each out breath. Once you feel really grounded begin to notice energy in other parts of your body.

Notice where you feel heavy, where you feel light, where you feel spacious, where you feel compression, where you feel warmth, and where you feel coolness. Allow your energies to rise from your feet, imagining this energy being free to move all the way up through your spine, your shoulders, neck and head, to the sky. Work creatively in sensing this connection between earth and sky. After exploring this connection for a few minutes, notice your energy and any thoughts, feelings, and body memories which arise.

Gradually bring your attention more fully to your lower body and to your shoulders. Listen carefully and tenderly, noticing any clenching, constriction, tension or pressure in these areas. Kindly breathe space and loving-kindness into these areas, allowing them to relax on your out breath.

Notice the outward shape and form of your lower torso, particularly the area around your hips and buttocks. Take as much time as you wish in paying kindly attention to the shape and feel of these areas. Feel where your body makes contact with your chair or cushion, feeling supported and able to relax into a sense of being held. Notice the front, back and sides of your lower torso, noticing any areas that feel a bit cramped or contracted or held in, stretching and creating more space where you can. Pay attention to how you hold yourself in this region. Perhaps experiment with tensing and releasing your lower stomach muscles and your buttocks in turn, noticing the tension and release. Do the same with your shoulders, perhaps tensing your shoulders up towards your ears, and then releasing them. Push your shoulders downwards, and then release, allowing them to find their own natural level.

Explore your lower torso with an inward awareness. Begin by contacting a sense of kindness as you gently use your breath as a way of breathing space and air down into your lower abdomen and, as you release, allow a sense of relaxation. Imagine breathing into all the corners and cavities of your lower torso, and all the way up into your shoulders, imagining the inside of your body as a great cathedral spire or dome, stretching up from mighty foundations. Try this for several minutes, allowing your breath to follow its own pace and depth. Notice the rising and falling of your diaphragm as you breathe, feeling the motion throughout your torso, tracking the flow of energy from your earthed base to your head, in a skyward direction. Enjoy any sensations of spaciousness and well-being as you sit, being aware of thoughts, feelings, memories and images. As you gently and slowly bring the meditation to a close, extend these feelings of well-being outwards, spreading to all parts of your body. Invite a sense of appreciation and gratitude for yourself, for making the effort to spend time with your body, breath and felt senses.

The thrusting character position

Turning towards meditation

The chances are that those of us with thrusting character patterning will think that meditation is a wishy-washy activity practised by alternative people. After all, we probably think of ourselves as too busy and focused to take time to relax. If, and when, we realise that meditation brings its own challenges (not least, the challenge of sitting with the unpredictability of our own bodies and minds – we might be surprised to find that our mind is not *quite* as focused as we believed it to be) we might be more inclined to develop greater respect for the art of meditation. In realising this, it is possible that we may engage in a battle of wills with ourselves, aiming for the clearest, most concentrated meditations possible. We may also be competitive in comparing our experiences in meditation with those around us.

We apply the same approach to meditation as to any other activity: winning, striving, conquering. Given that meditation is about sitting still and finding out 'who's at home', it is unlikely that many of us with this patterning will be naturally drawn to meditation. For a boundary character, meditation can be another curious way of entering unexplored realms of consciousness. For a thrusting character, other realms of consciousness are likely to be seen as a way-out alien idea, given that there is enough to be doing and achieving here in the 'real world'.

It is also unlikely that those of us with this patterning are drawn to meditation in the course of our everyday lives, though there are exceptions. We might have been recommended to learn meditation by our doctor, perhaps to help us with a particular medical condition (perhaps high blood pressure, insomnia or a persistent back problem). We might also have heard that meditation is a good way to train and tame our minds, which we may find appealing as a means to perfecting our sporting or work performance.

In learning meditation it is useful to find a teacher who can meet fully our questions and challenges. This relationship has the potential to be significant and reparative. If we meet someone who can meet us 'head-on', without being thrown or wrong-footed by our very direct, penetrating, most likely combative approach, they are likely to win our respect. This may make it more likely for us to stay engaged with meditation over a longer time period.

The benefits of meditation

One of the most important benefits of meditation is that it potentially offers us the chance to stop and be present, rather than constantly striving and pushing forwards. If we can sustain our meditation practice we are likely to start to see just how much energy it takes us to constantly strive to win. As a result we might give ourselves permission to take an occasional break, giving us a glimpse of how it might be to live with a greater sense of balance and paying more attention to our body rather than treating it like a machine to be operated at full capacity.

In the longer-term meditation can help us to become clearer about how we approach communication and relationships, in particular, how we seek to be the 'winner' in the course of our interactions with others. If we let ourselves see this pattern and notice our dynamics, we start to see how much energy we expend in living life competitively. Identifying this strategy might be experienced as both a relief and a source of deep confusion. We are likely to need to make considerable adjustments in culti-vating awareness around this patterning, moving between our default way of approaching life and seeing these strategies with a deeper, softer awareness.

For those of us who resonate with the thrusting character position, becoming more self-aware could mean we become something of a force to be reckoned with, in terms of our huge potential for engaged and embodied positive actions in the world! How this manifests will, of course, vary from person to person. In 'spiritual' terms, it has the potential to give us an intense sense of focus, vision and steely determination in practising meditation – we will not easily be distracted from our mission.

Working edges

The most significant working edge that we are initially likely to encounter is the challenge of sticking with meditation for long enough to realise its benefits. In fact, it might be difficult for us to get our heads around why anyone would choose to sit still, with their eyes shut, in a roomful of people focusing on their breath for half an hour. This reminds me of a day I was teaching meditation to a class of sixteen-year-old students. One high-energy, determined, focused young man decided to check his text and emails in the middle of the meditation. He said after-wards that it would have been unthinkable to have broken contact with the outside world for a whole half an hour. Perhaps this young man was a thrusting character, making sure he was not missing out on more pressing business happening in his everyday life.

Presuming we do stick around and engage fully with meditation, the strongest working edge we are likely to encounter is having the emotional honesty to face the reasons why we set the bar of achievement so high. As we face this we will also start to come into relationship with our inner exhaustion of rarely allowing any sense of human fallibility or vulnerability to rise to the foreground of our experience. It is incredibly challenging for us to experience this, let alone share it with others. Realising and sitting with this new sense of fallibility could be a make or break point in our deepening self awareness.

We may tend towards two poles in response to this realisation. We may either walk away from meditation, claiming that it clearly does not work, or become overconfident. We may be pretty driven in pushing ourselves to make breakthroughs in meditation, in a wilful way, leaving large parts of ourselves behind, particularly our softer, more vulnerable parts which rarely get a look in.

If we continue meditating, we are likely to approach it with a boom or bust attitude. We may be very wilful, pitting ourselves against our limitations, as a way of reinforcing old habits and as a way of keeping vulnerability at bay. Whilst there is merit in engaging effort, it might be a challenge for us to practise with the Buddhist notion of 'balanced effort', the sixth stage of the Buddhist 'Noble Eightfold Path' (see Bodhi, 1994 and Sangharakshita, 1990). The consequence of being over-wilful in meditation (apart from giving ourselves a headache, sore shoulders and a tight belly) is that our focus becomes wilfulness, rather than a state of alert relaxation focusing upon the object of the meditation. A working edge will be getting interested in noticing when we are being overwilful, for example, doing the wilful 'bhavana' rather than the 'metta bhavana' or loving-kindness meditation.

We might also think we have 'got' things prematurely, seeing states of mind as absolute end states, given that we live life with striving and achievement in mind. I am reminded of a conversation with a friend. He pronounced, boldly and proudly, "I finally understand going for refuge." I was struck by this, given that my friend had only been practising Buddhism for a very short time. I also (secretly) admired his bold, rather black and white bravado. I was reminded of how different our styles are, in approaching life and practice. Whilst his approach is very different to mine, this thrusting way will be his particular approach and the habits he will be working with this lifetime.

In my mind this is the beauty of understanding character positions. In making sense of our experience and style through character, we can work *with* – rather than against – our resistances, transforming the energy driving them. In doing this, we avoid entering into a pointless fight with ourselves, of either making ourselves right or wrong, or in relentlessly comparing ourselves to others. It is also vital to bear in mind that each character position has a very creative aspect once we have given ourselves the opportunity to come into relationship with those aspects of character which need a bit of attention, reality testing and updating.

In meditating, our body as a thrusting character will benefit from allowing in a greater softness and a rest from our rigid, taut sense of 'uprightness'. It is likely to be a long-term project for us to be able to feel, acknowledge and be at ease with a sense of softness and vulnerability. It can be very difficult for us to know what to do with this sense of softness, apart from feeling profoundly awkward and in very unfamiliar territory. In facing and practising with these working edges, it will be very useful if we meet a meditation teacher who can meet our energy and questions in a head-on energetic way. This could be an important factor in determining whether we return for week two of our meditation course.

Engaging our energy fully before meditation will be useful preparation. Other supports for our meditation practice might include walking meditation, movement, or the martial arts, as a way of making the transition to meditation. By noticing our physical senses in this way, we are likely to give ourselves a better chance to learn to start to listen to our bodymind, rather than setting it a challenge, and continuing to relate to our bodies in a more objectified way. Walking meditation may particularly suit us as we will still be in touch with the sense of 'uprightness' which matters so much.

Learning Buddhist teachings is a useful way to set meditation in its wider context and engage our energies. There are several stories of headstrong individuals wishing to break through, with which we may resonate. There are also teachings which throw light on the need for different qualities in living and practising, for example, the 'five spiritual faculties' (see Sangharakshita, 1998: 144-161).

These five faculties are: wisdom, faith, energy, concentration and mindfulness. Wisdom is balanced with faith, which is about balancing our capacity for true understanding with a more devotional approach. Energy in pursuit of the good is balanced with concentration and one-pointedness of mind, which is about balancing our capacity for engaged activity with sitting still and focusing. Both of these pairs are balanced on the fulcrum of mindfulness. This fulcrum can provide balance, so that the bodymind is not pulled to extremes, instead the fulcrum holds the creative tension between the poles of wisdom and faith, energy and concentration. The beauty of this teaching is that it shows us how no particular quality is more important than another, but rather that they are complemented by one another.

Reflections and meditation exercises

Review what you have noted in reading this chapter. Begin by reflecting on the following pairs in the way you live life and approach your meditation practice:

Creating/destroying, strong/weak, winning/losing, fixing/breaking, succeeding/failing, upright/spineless, hero/fool, industrious/lazy.

Walking meditation:

Explore walking meditation. Set aside twenty minutes in a garden or large room where you can walk in a circle, clockwise. Make sure you are undisturbed. Begin by simply starting to walk at a pace which feels right. Take in your surroundings: what you see as you walk, noises, the temperature. When you have been walking for a few minutes start to focus upon the weight of your body on each of your feet as your weight moves from your left foot to your right foot. Notice the different parts of your feet as your weight shifts – your toes right through to your heel.

After walking for a while start to notice the cycle of your breath in and out of your body. Pay attention to where the air enters your body, the shape of its overall cycle through your body, and where you sense your out breath. Let the flow of your breath be as natural as possible, rather than controlling it. In following your breath notice your mood and your general energy levels.

Start to scan your body from head to foot. As you walk notice where you feel more or less energised and where it takes more or less effort to stay upright. Pay attention to areas of your body which feel well, energised, and relaxed, as well as the areas where you notice more tension. Continue to walk and focus upon different dimensions of your experience, for example, your breath, the changing weight on your feet, and your changing contact with the ground.

As you move towards the end of the meditation period start to broaden your awareness to again include your surroundings. At the end of the walking meditation session, stand still for a few minutes to notice fully how you feel. Compare how you felt at the beginning of the walking with how you are now. Notice where you feel energised, heavier, lighter, focused, diffused, warmer and cooler.

The more you practise walking meditation the more successful you will be in noticing ever more subtle sensations in your body and its movement.

Meditation exploring your lower back, pelvis, and shoulders:

Set up your meditation conditions so you arrive and are as present and relaxed as possible, perhaps beginning with a full body awareness meditation or the walking meditation as suggested above. Make sure you will be undisturbed, unplug the phone and switch off your mobile phone.

Begin by noticing the shape of your overall form on your meditation cushion. Notice your head, neck and shoulders. Allow your head to feel poised upon your shoulders in a state of relaxed alertness, rather than held rigidly or tensely. Notice the shape of your arms, belly, hips and bottom. Pay attention to how you hold yourself in this area, inviting a greater sense of relaxation and softening where you can. Make sure your arms are supported by a cushion or blanket, giving your shoulders and upper arms a chance to relax fully. Bring your awareness to the shape of your legs, seated in meditation posture. As you breathe, allow your legs to soften and sink into the ground. Notice where your energy flows in your body and any thoughts, sensations and resistances which arise. Pay attention to the ebb and flow of your breath, following its pace and depth with a sense of acceptance. Also follow the movement of your breath as you apply an attentive awareness. Starting from your head and shoulders and working downwards, imagine your breath bringing a sense of softening and relaxation through the whole of your body. Pay particular attention to the areas of tension you discovered in your earlier walking meditation. Imagine your breath reaching up into the base of your skull and, as you breathe out, the breath bringing a wave of softening down through your upper body, and all the way through your lower body.

Continue with this breathing, paying attention to areas which welcome this sense of spacious softening, all the way down to your feet and toes. If you feel sufficiently relaxed in these gentle movements of your breath and body, allow your body to move from an upright, seated position, to a lying down position, allowing your body to fully relax, guided by the regular beat and rhythm of your breath. In lying down make sure you have the support of cushions and a blanket.

As you continue to sit or lie down in meditation invite your breath to pay particular attention to the areas around your lower back, pelvis and shoulders. Imagine your breath bringing energy and support to these areas, so you feel relaxed and revitalised as you breathe. Get a sense of the shape of your body in this area outwardly and inwardly. Notice what you find in these areas: well-being, tension, sensations and memories. Spend as long as you want bringing awareness to these areas, allowing them to rest and sink, giving way to the force of gravity, and supported by the earth. When you start to bring the meditation to a close, imagine any tensions in your lower back, pelvis, and shoulders being dispersed into the earth to be recycled, breathing in the sense of rest spreading throughout your body.

The crisis character position
Turning towards meditation
Patterned by the crisis character position, we are likely to seek to learn meditation as a way of cultivating a greater sense of peace and calm in our everyday experience. Fear and panic are the emotions underlying much of our experience. Anything that helps to bring this fear and panic into more conscious awareness

is invaluable. In the short-term our purpose might be crisis management. In the longer-term, we might become adept at identifying how we habitually create crisis conditions, or respond with drama.

Early on in meditating we may get a sense of gathering together our energies, learning to sit still: quietly and alone. This might be the first time that some of us have sat completely alone for any period of time, so it is likely at first to feel very unfamiliar and unsettling. As this experience becomes more familiar, we will start to feel more physically and energetically 'anchored'. This might reflect back to us how our energy in everyday life zooms around our bodies, seeking constant expression, at a breakneck pace. Experiencing this new sense of being anchored will provide a welcome contrast.

Given the nature of our everyday zooming energy, we are soon likely to encounter challenges in sitting with ourselves for any length of time. An early challenge is likely to be when we touch a new, unfamiliar sense of intimacy with ourselves. In this scenario, or perhaps in contacting other fears, we might leave our meditation cushion and jump to our feet before we even know what has happened. This is the hindrance of restlessness and anxiety par excellence. It reflects the speed at which we generally operate and process. Left to our own devices we rarely leave a breathing space between initial thought and action, which is a way of being on our guard and always being ready to respond to stimuli. This can be a real benefit in some situations; but during a meditation session, it is likely to be an obstacle, actual or potential.

Not having a captive audience during meditation can also be challenging. Whilst those of us with control character patterning may feel bereft at not having others around to shape and manage, as a crisis character we will falter in not having an audience to enchant, entertain, charm, and seduce. Remember from earlier that this is the way we gain attention as a way of avoiding more authentic contact with ourselves and others. On the one hand, we may experience huge relief in not having to be the resident performer, and, on the other, we may quickly feel bored and lost, not really knowing who we are and what we are supposed to be doing. Not only will we have no audience, but if we are new to meditation, we will also be at a loss to know the rules. We are likely to find these two factors seriously disorienting.

We will need to learn how to ground ourselves at the beginning of every session of meditation, making ourselves as physically comfortable as possible. In terms of the traditional hindrances to meditation, we are likely to find that we work with restlessness and anxiety and sense desire, rather than sloth and torpor. It is important that we take time to settle and arrive in meditation: in the room, on the cushion and relaxing into our posture. We will need to check in with ourselves briefly, contacting our sense of purpose and contracting with ourselves how long we plan to spend sitting, and sticking to that plan.

The benefits of meditation

Our habitual way of relating is to appear as fascinating and as charming as we possibly can, as a way of making ourselves acceptable in the world. We have lively energy and can exude a sense of 'loved-up' magnetism. If we are also patterned by the oral character position, this is likely to be heightened by our quality of being very endearing. Energetically, this is quite a contrast with the stereotypical image of a meditating Buddha: calm, rooted and contented. Consequently, meditation can be incredibly beneficial in encouraging us to engage more fully with everyday life and what we find in front of us in each moment, rather than distracting ourselves and providing enter-tainment and drama. Our fascination with life and relationship can pay dividends in taking us deeper in meditation, delving into deeper relationship with ourselves and the world, if we have sufficient patience and persistence to at first gather ourselves and to quieten our energies.

Quietening, calming and stilling are the most obvious benefits of meditation for the crisis character. On the level of engaging with meditation as a relaxation exercise, it will provide us with 'time out' from our habitual sense of excitement and fear. We will get a stronger sense of when our overwhelm button is about to be pressed (by ourselves or others). We will also start to become freer to choose how to respond – do we want to go headlong into full drama – running the risk of ending up in an exhausted heap – or do we want to notice what is happening and try something different?

Meditation will invite us into fuller contact with our bodies, as they are, without demands to entertain or be anything in particular (sexy, attractive, beautiful…) Being focused upon our bodies and breath in meditation can, at first at least, be very challenging indeed, for the reasons explored. As we enter into a fuller relationship with our embodiment we are likely to experience relief and a greater sense of wholeness. We might get a sense, perhaps for the first time, that we have access to a more conscious choice about who we are and what we do, particularly with regards to our bodies. We need to be kindly in our approach, given that in reflecting and meditating upon our embodiment we give ourselves the chance to process fully events and experiences remembered by our body.

It is likely that a longer-term process in meditation will be about us reclaiming our sense of being a body, and enjoying being a body, in a healthy, human way. This is likely to be about being with a sense of embodiment on our own terms, rather than in relationship to the needs, wishes, approval, or abuse of others, which will have been a defining dynamic in our conditioning. This will be a very beneficial aspect of meditation, giving us the ability to be with ourselves in a much quieter, calmer, more accepting way. If meditation can support those of us patterned by boundary character patterning to realise we *are* a bodymind on earth, for those of us with crisis character patterning meditation conditions will give us the chance to realise that we do have a choice of what to do with our bodies and our energies. Channelling our energy into our 'spiritual' practice might be a very reparative and wholesome process.

As we become more experienced in meditation we are likely to have a great capacity to play with the rules creatively, finding numerous ways to get into our meditation practice, relating to ourselves, and working effectively with hindrances. I am reminded of a friend, shaped by the oral and crisis character positions, and her creative work in meditation:

> In meditation I have a very creative dialogue with myself, which is very visual. I see pictures in my mind's eye. In starting to meditate I use visualisation to cultivate a calm state. Then the images take over: I surrender to them. This becomes what I call a 'bubbling up' meditation – a very strong experience – a 'peg' for my practice. Meditations like this contain deep insights about where I'm at. I'm aware as I speak that I'm quite excited about these meditations! They're a koan too – they can fuel and nourish meditation and they can run away with me. I need to come back to simplicity and focus. Having meditations like this is a capacity I have, which I need to honour.

Working edges

The koan mentioned above by my friend is likely to be a strong working edge for many of us as crisis characters. We will sometimes find ourselves dancing on a tightrope between using our energy creatively in meditation, and getting lost in fantasy. On less creative days, it is likely that we will find it virtually impossible to make the space and time to sit down in silence, contemplating our breath for half an hour. Sitting might at times seem unbearable: a study in embodied pain. There are a number of reasons for this.

Firstly, the tendencies and preferences of this particular character armouring mean that we are unlikely to be drawn to sitting still and alone. Secondly, in sitting alone and still, we have the opportunity, perhaps for the first time, to see how much we are driven by panic and the physicality of that panic. Seeing this can be daunting, as well as a relief. We might also contact or re-contact scary and painful body memories and might well need the support of others in coming to terms with these memories, thoughts and feelings. Thirdly, as a direct response to seeing the zooming, panicky energy within, we may find it too challenging to sit back down on our meditation cushion.

A vicious circle can ensue. Whilst we know that meditating is valuable and illuminating, the thought of it may be too challenging. Over time, our practice in working with this edge might be about coming back to calming and grounding ourselves and doing a period of the mindfulness of breathing. Or on other occasions we are likely to simply be bored by meditation. Perhaps we have run out of distracting ways of entertaining ourselves in meditation and we miss the audience we can normally whip up in everyday life. Working with boredom and restlessness may be a recurring challenge as we go deeper.

One aspect we are likely to find supportive in working in meditation is sharing our experiences with others. We are likely to be very entertaining in regaling other meditators with our vivid experiences. This is a positive thing in that we can enlist the help of those around us to dialogue about our experience, thereby normalising rather than dramatising experiences, and not feeling so alone with the process of meditation. Our attraction to relating to others, as a crisis character, can be a real strength in this way, so long as we don't simply become the stand-up meditation comedian, entertaining rather than really communi-cating with others about our experience.

Another aspect supportive to meditation is creating a physical space in which we will not be disturbed. Creating this physical space can help us to make the transition between activities, and provide us with a visual reminder of our purpose. For some of us this space might be meditating at a class. In meditating at a class bear in mind the importance of managing well the transitions between relating to others before meditation, and turning inwards for the meditation session itself. It can be invaluable to be conscious of keeping our energies grounded as we arrive at the class, otherwise we are likely to spend a fair amount of the meditation session simply bringing our energy back to earth, after stimulating interactions.

We might also find we are distracted by falling in love with those around us – we have a great capacity for this – or, on the opposite pole, we might disappear into our androgynous shell and feel unable to be ourselves in any real sense. Learning to be aware of our different energies can be a very creative process in surrendering to meditation, if we give ourselves the necessary time and attention. Our energy as a creative crisis character position can be irresistible, leading others to also fall in love with meditation and practice. We have the potential to be an embodied exemplar of the 'rite of fascination'; our warmth and play drawing others to tread the path of practice.

Reflections and meditation exercises

Give yourself time to notice what 'jumped off the page' as you read this chapter. Begin by reflecting on the following pairs in the way you live, and in your approach to meditation:

Hiding/showing, fascinating/dull, attracting/repelling, entertaining/boring, noisy/quiet, spinning/still point, lively/lifeless, closing/opening.

Moving into meditation

Try moving into meditation through beginning with body movement. This might be useful if you are feeling particularly 'buzzy' and need some sort of transition from everyday activity into meditation. In this way you can harness your exuberant energy, rather than suppressing it. In moving into meditation, you might find that the dance between movement and stillness, and back to movement, closely echoes your internal process and movement of energy, giving you the chance to attune with yourself before meditation.

Rather than dancing in a more conventional sense, give yourself the permission to move your body in the way it really wishes to move. You might be more used to performing or dancing in a more stylised way, so give yourself plenty of time, allowing your energies to settle and quieten down. Turn inwards gently and tenderly as you stand, sit or lie down. It might take some time to settle into this and to really tune in to your internal weather. You may have a tussle with coyness or self consciousness or performing, even when you are alone.

Pay close attention to your breath, your body on the ground, and the energy of your heart, as you listen to how your body wants to move, stretch, curl up, gather inwards, or move in whatever way it chooses. Try to follow the movement from within, rather than to let an idea or thought take over and do something for you. When you notice a disconnection from your breath and embodied sense come back to this and start moving again, with love and patience. Come back to your in breath and slowly follow how it moves through your body. Do this for as long as possible as a preparation for sitting meditation.

Meditation exploring your pelvis and thighs:

Take time to settle into your meditation posture, perhaps through moving (as above) or through some devotional practice. Starting with your head and, working downwards, notice the nature of your energy. Pay attention to where you notice energy in your body, whether it is high or low, darting around or more or less settled and notice where you feel more stimulated and energised.

Spend as much time as possible getting really curious about your energy and your relationship with it. Notice your responses as you explore, following your energy at its own pace and on its own pathway, as it moves through your body. Take care to give this exploration your full attention, away from the world, taking time out to learn more about your embodied experience.

Now notice the overall shape of your form. Do this in as embodied a way as possible, sensing your form, rather than seeing yourself as you think others see you. Paint a picture in your mind's eye, or kinaesthetically notice what it is like to be your body with its particular shape, size, weight, and the space your body and energy occupy. Notice pleasurable and painful feelings. Take as much notice of the areas which feel dull, uninteresting or a little numb and let them share any memories, thoughts or feelings.

From your head downwards, allow your energies to settle and take 'time out' to be still and rested. Imagine waves of gentle, soothing energy flowing through you as you breathe in and breathe out. Use your breath as a kindly way into your embodied experience. The breath can act as an anchor as you bring a gentle softening to each of the areas of your body: head, neck, shoulders, arms, hands, chest, belly, hips, bottom, thighs, knees, calves, ankles, feet, toes.

Allow this softening at its own pace, perhaps spending more time on certain areas of the body. Be kindly as you explore, breathing in gentle kindness to areas which feel uncertain, hesitant, or restless. Stay with what you are doing, with a gentle sense of purpose, giving yourself the chance to feel this softening. Notice where you feel heavy, light, hot, cold, stretched, hidden, rested and strung out. Attend to each area and sensation with a compassionate awareness.

Once you have scanned your whole body, allow your softening breath to pay particular attention to the area around your pelvis, belly, bottom and thighs. Imagine the shape of this area, breathing in spaciousness, and surrendering any tensions to the gathering sense of softness in your body awareness. It might be useful to place your hands on your belly and heart centre as you relax.

Allow the busy muscles in your belly and thighs to soften and become as heavy as possible, giving in to gravity. Imagine a freeing of any energy held in this lower half of your body. Perhaps visualise tensions softening, moving from taut and tight to melting, softening and opening. Move gently and respectfully in this exploration, entering into a kindly dialogue with yourself, working at your own pace and following your own impulses. As you slowly and kindly bring the meditation to a close, allow the sense of well-being in this softening to permeate as much of your experience as possible. Give yourself as much time as possible to absorb and assimilate this feeling before moving into your next activity.

Conclusion

My work in introducing character positions is almost complete as this book draws to a close. By means of completion I shall end with a few comments about what I have learned in applying character to my practice of meditation. I hope that these thoughts encourage you to continue to experiment in reflecting upon the relationship between your embodying and your meditation practice, making your own discoveries.

Staying really curious

The invitation of this book has been to encourage you to become more curious about your experience of being a body, to explore what goes on during meditation, and to understand your lifelong habits. I encourage you to continue to cultivate that sense of curiosity, which is vital, life-enhancing juice in supporting you to stay with your processes of both embodiment and meditation. Becoming really curious opens up a channel through which we can access information about our bodyminds which we might not be aware of in our everyday experience. At times when we feel less of a connection with curiosity and wonder, it is useful to remember the importance of friends and fellow meditators in helping us to re-ignite our touch paper of faith.

Committing to a process of discovering

It is impossible to know where meditation will take us. (If, in fact, there is anywhere 'to go'.) You can have endless ideas about meditation, and you can set your purpose, but it is, of course, impossible to know your destination, or even the mooring points along the way. Nor can you be sure what it will mean to be more in touch with being a body. The more you reflect upon Buddhist teachings, the more likely it becomes that the notions of 'I', 'me', and 'mine' are less and less relevant as points of reference. You might find that it can be a bit of a tussle surrendering to a more expansive, less 'me'-focused sense of being. You might sway between determinedly hanging on to a more fixed idea of your 'self' some days, and enjoy blissful limitlessness on others, perhaps depending upon how strongly the worldly winds are blowing. In the spirit of the beginning of this book, you can always start from where you find yourself, recommitting to the process of discovery which is meditation.

Attending to loving-kindness (metta) and mindfulness

As you explore more about character and meditation it is useful to keep a strong connection with your regular meditation practices. Keep doing the practices which work for you, given that they provide the foundation for experimentation. Practising loving-kindness meditations can be useful in providing emotional robustness, in parallel with attuning to a deeper sensitivity. Practising mindfulness meditation can bring clarity and integration. Just sitting and less form-based meditations can provide the opportunity to assimilate your experience and cultivate receptivity.

Sustaining a meditation practice and exploring embodiment take time, patience, and loving-kindness (rather like sustaining a friendship or love affair). You might channel loving-kindness during meditation, as well as from the support of friends. In the spirit of interconnection stay in touch with your friends and fellow meditators as you practise, given that inspiration seems to be contagious, rather than something which you can artificially conjure up.

Loving the messy bits

To become more embodied is to develop a more compassionate and kindly dialogue with the messy, more stubborn, and resistant bits of your experience. I am reminded of the title of the book by Jack Kornfield, *After the Ecstasy, the Laundry*, (Kornfield, 2000). In meditating and exploring your embodiment you are likely to become much more familiar with your 'laundry' and your version of 'inner messiness'. This might emerge as a particular theme, as a persuasive resistance, or as a life struggle with which you are all too familiar, experienced in a more embodied way. Messy bits can often be veiled in shame, covered by clever strategies or can have a knack of fogging your awareness as you draw closer. A very real and painful struggle can then ensue between the bits of you that are happy enough with the status quo, and the bits planning something of an internal coup d'etat.

This sense of messiness might be a particularly sensitively-experienced issue for those of you who resonate with the holding character, for the reasons explored earlier. It might present itself as a conundrum to boundary characters. Those of you with this patterning might try to figure it out in a similar vein to solving a maths puzzle, with perhaps limited results. Crisis characters might leap in and play around in the mess, learning the rules and breaking them. Whatever character positions you recognise in your experience, you are likely to work most effectively with this inner messiness by calling forth the creative aspects of your character conditioning and developing strategies that help you to witness your process and stay engaged.

As good as it gets

The more I meditate and become aware of the dynamics of my embodiment, the more frequently I am struck by the very ordinary flavour of moments of quite deep contentment. I am struck by the magic of everyday things: green shoots pushing determinedly from the earth in late winter, a friend's kind act, and the beauty of a view which I might pass everyday, but often fail to really *see*. Perhaps this appreciation of the ordinary flavour of contentment is sparked by feeling a greater sense of ease in being a body, with more space to breathe, feeling the effects of gravity, and not feeling so confined in our own skin.

This greater spaciousness is a bit like the effect of being absorbed in a relaxed, alert state of meditation. The ways in which you become aware of your states of mind are related to your particular character patterning. Understanding your character patterns and strategies can help you to see your habitual patterning, to enjoy its creative manifestations and to set up the conditions so that you enjoy the fruits: the ordinary magic of moments of contentment and connection.

Self and other, this life and past lives

Looking at character positions in any depth brings to light interesting questions as to how and why you found particular developmental stages difficult in being conceived, born and growing up this lifetime. It is pretty likely that you are shaped by character positions according to the particular volitions with which you arrived in this particular lifetime. This is a fascinating area of reflection from a Buddhist perspective, from the point of view of karma (literally translated as 'action') and rebirth.

There are specific areas of my own conditioning which certainly feel like they were shaped many lifetimes ago. Some of my habits seem *so* deeply entrenched. The more I become aware of my conditioning and its effects and dynamics this lifetime, the stronger I get the sense that I have been working with these habits for several lifetimes. It can be useful to reflect anew on rebirth, in attending to those patterns and tendencies which perhaps reinforce particular grooves and patterns from past lives.

Celebrating the creative aspects of character

Exploring character positions is about honouring your journey so far: the rich soil from which you and your life (or lives) have grown, like the shoots of a lotus plant pushing its way through the mud and silt of the lake floor. Reflecting on character as presented in this book is not intended to be about making wrong, typecasting or fixing yourself or others. Seeing with character positions in mind gives you the chance to celebrate who you are and what you have learned. There is often little opportunity to take stock in the current mainstream climate, with a lack of the marking of important life events through rituals, rites of passage and celebrations. It seems a shame that it is generally only at funerals that we feel free to speak with gratitude and appreciation about those we love. Let us bring back appreciating each other, as often as is humanly possible!

Psychological v 'spiritual'?

This book spans the areas of psychology and 'spirituality'. In this way it feels risky, in as much as it brings together areas which have not so far been brought together in this very particular way (so far as I am aware). It is a live experiment in seeing how a working awareness of character positions supports your practice as a meditator. I sometimes hear fellow Buddhist practitioners judge things as 'a bit too psychological'. I imagine that they mean that a specifically 'spiritual' dimension is missing. It is not a judgement I generally find myself making, mainly because my 'spiritual' practice has been informed by information and ideas from so many different arenas – some rather unexpected.

I hope character positions are not written off as 'too psychological' in this arena. Drawing upon the framework of character positions offers the chance to explore patterns and dynamics from your responses at key development stages of your life, and from past lives, as a means of setting up the best conditions for practice in your current life. Understanding character positions can throw light on our conditioning and help us to explore difference. Character can help us to see the strategies we have adopted in making it possible to be a living, breathing human being, facing life's inevitable imperfections and beauty. Character positions help to illustrate how we have become the character we are today, in all our rich complexity and simplicity.

With character in mind, I am reminded of the parable of the rain cloud, from the White Lotus Sutra (Soothill, 1994). In this sutra rain clouds shower refreshing rain upon all the earth's plants. In a similar way, the Buddha teaches the Dharma to all living beings. This 'Dharma rain' falls equally on all beings, without discrimination. As Sangharakshita points out, each plant grows and blossoms in its own way, each with its own distinctive beauty and character (Sangharakshita, 1998: 26).

In my mind this is analogous to how each Buddha and bodhisattva has his or her own distinct character and qualities, whilst sharing the experience of being enlightened. I often remind myself of this: 'spiritual' practice is about becoming more and more enlightened from the starting point of who you are today, with your personality, qualities and character. In becoming more enlightened and insightful, you become more yourself. (And on this theme, words start to fall short...)

What might become less recognisable – at least from an everyday human point of view – is your extraordinary compassion and awesome wisdom as an enlightened being, still expressed in, and through, your current character and qualities. Enlightenment is not a bland state of homogeneity, but (I imagine!) – a rich pantheon of Buddhas and bodhisattvas of different shapes, colours, energies and forms. I am rather fond of this parable. It reminds me of the marriage between the ordinary and the profound, between the psychological and the 'spiritual', between the understanding of enlightenment as 'in here' and 'out there'.

Shedding old skins

Exploring character positions in the context of meditation can be a practice of shedding old skins. As you 'tune in' more fully and listen to your experience, you would be hard pushed to fail to notice your more creative and more limiting moments of expression. Seeing the more and less helpful aspects of your patterning can be immensely illuminating.

What you do with that illumination will vary according to your particular character and purpose. Shedding old skins – outgrown skins – calls for an emerging sense of receptivity and surrender as you create the conditions to loosen your attachment to the views, feelings, sensations and behaviours associated with the denying and yearning aspects of a particular character position. This process cannot be rushed and cannot be planned, but calls for effort, patience, perseverance and love.

Those of you reading who have embarked on a journey or path of 'spirituality' will be acutely aware that it is one thing to identify and fully experience a particular habit, and another to know what to do with it. Whilst your habits and resistances might drive you a bit crazy, there can also be a sense of holding on to them, because at least they are familiar. For many there is likely to be a sense of comfort in that familiarity, even though the habit itself can be counterproductive and pain-inducing. Shedding old skins calls for courage, emotional honesty and curiosity about what might be on the horizon.

The interface between the public and private spheres

Meditation and embodiment are interesting areas in that they both operate in a private sphere in many ways, yet have wider, much more public consequences. Some of these themes were explored in Chapter 4. Engaging with loving-kindness meditation – bringing to mind all those different living beings, in the context of meditation – has an effect. This might be a quite tangible effect of feeling more loving-kindness towards a friend when you see them later that day, through to an effect more akin to the healing power of contemplation. Similarly, your relationship with your body is, in one way, intensely personal, yet is so shaped by your interconnections with others and a multitude of events and phenomena. How you treat your body and how that impacts upon others is very significant, yet so often overlooked.

Reflecting upon character positions in the context of developing your meditation practice can be useful in terms of integrating the very solitary sense of sitting alone in meditation, yet being more acutely aware of your connections with other – past and present – through different facets of your character positions. I am reminded of the title of Stephen Batchelor's thought-provoking book, *Alone with Others* (Batchelor, 1983). In meditating you sit alone, whether you sit in a shrine room or at home. Exploring meditation from the point of view of character positions can help you to make sense of your meditation practice to date, your related place in the world and your place in the continuing flow of phenomena.

Learning from and learning about

There is a difference between learning *from* your bodymind and learning *about* your bodymind. This difference is like the shift required for us collectively to learn *from* the planet, rather than to learn *about* it, thinking we are mistresses and masters of the universe, without really taking time to learn *from* our environment (and to let it teach us). I would like to draw an analogy from my practice of Buddhism. Earlier on I mentioned the centrality of 'going for refuge' at the point of ordination as a Buddhist. 'Going for refuge to the three jewels' consists of continually orienting my life and practice towards the Buddha, Dharma (teachings) and Sangha ('spiritual' fellowship).

In terms of going for refuge, this learning *from* as well as learning *about* is significant. I learn *from* the Buddha, Dharma, and Sangha – the three mighty jewels of Buddhism – through inviting them into the heart of my life and practice, rather than simply attempting to learn *about* them in a drier, somehow more intellectual or academic way. Deepening your meditation calls for this learning *from*, as well as *about*. Meditation needs clear instruction, balanced effort and discipline, as well as the greater 'moistness' and juice of poetry, myth and magic. Many different ingredients are needed to nurture your practice, some of them not always immediately obvious or predictable.

If all else fails – relax

Finally, I am reminded again of the words of Achalavajra, my first meditation teacher. He would introduce eloquently the particular meditation practice he was leading during a class. Often, he would then smile, sit back, and say, "If all else fails and you forget what I've said, just relax!" This is great advice – sometimes difficult to put into practise, but well worth remembering. Thinking about character positions and getting clear about your purpose might sometimes feel all too much. At that point, remember Achalavajra's words and come back to your breath and your earth-touching base.

Healing happens as and when

Practising meditation and actively exploring embodiment brings healing and greater wholeness. Healing can mean many different things to different people. In this context I mean the way in which the energies of your bodymind can be freer to express themselves. This, in turn, enables you to live more authentically. In casting the light of awareness on your practice of meditation and embodying, you are setting up the best conditions for healing to take place, at its own time and pace.

This healing may take the form of the softening and dissolving of body armouring, so its limitations are not quite so constricting. It might mean being prepared to be with and witness a grieving process about a particular event or phase of your life which has not been able to happen until this point. It might be about allowing the full expression of a particular quality you embody, a little less shackled by the voices of fear and doubt.

As far as I can tell in my own experience, and in working

therapeutically with others, making the space for healing to happen is greatly helped by being more aware of our inner controller, inner manager, inner organiser or whatever we can most aptly label the inner part of ourselves which is insistent on shaping, planning, controlling, putting right, or fixing. These busy inner organisers seem pretty familiar to most people I come across, and are perhaps accentuated in those for whom the control character position is prominent. Managing, organising – all these skills are really important and useful in life. They can be really useful in creating supportive conditions to sustain an effective meditation practice. They can also be so habitual, so much a part of our modus operandi, that they disallow the bodymind from processing and digesting in its own time and at its own pace.

'Spiritual' practitioners are, of course, not immune to this need to strive. I am put in mind of Chogyam Trungpa's notion of 'spiritual materialism' (Trungpa, 1973). Spiritual materialism describes the approach to 'spiritual' life which builds, rather than loosens, ego attachments, creating confusion and self-deception in 'spiritual' practitioners. Whilst we continue to approach meditation and embodying with this sense of striving we might be compromising the creation of conditions for healing. I often get a sense, particularly when I am really bargaining with life and reality – giving it a damn good shake – that if I could just stop doing this, I would be much closer to being more enlightened more of the time.

Life is full of itself. Life is mysterious. Life seeks to perpetuate life. This is an ordinary mystery, obvious to all of you with an ounce of curiosity and the awareness to realise that the world operates way beyond the control of your inner planner.

I will end with my favourite poem from Sangharakshita, with a great appreciation for his work as a translator and teacher of the Dharma. This poem says more eloquently what I am saying:

Hour after hour, day
After day we try
To grasp the Ungraspable, pinpoint
The Unpredictable. Flowers
Wither when touched, ice
Suddenly cracks beneath our feet. Vainly
We try to track birdflight through the sky, trace
Dumb fish through deep water, try
To anticipate the earned smile, the soft
Reward, even
Try to grasp our own lives. But Life
Slips through our fingers
Like snow. Life
Cannot belong to us. We
Belong to Life. Life
Is King.
Sangharakshita, 1995: 285

References

Analayo (2003) *Satipatthana: The Direct Path to Realization.* Windhorse Publications

Batchelor, S. (1983) *Alone With Others: An Existential Approach to Buddhism.* Grove Press, NY

Bodhi, Bhikkhu (1994) *The Noble Eightfold Path: Way to the End of Suffering.* Second edition. Buddhist Publication Society, Kandy, Sri Lanka

Bodhipaksa (2007) *Wildmind: A Step-by-Step Guide to Meditation.* Windhorse Publications

Bosnak, R. (1986) *A Little Course in Dreams: A basic handbook of Jungian dreamwork.* Shambhala Publications Inc, Boston & Shaftesbury

Brazier, D. (1995) *Zen Therapy: A Buddhist Approach to Psychotherapy.* Constable & Robinson Ltd, UK

Brown, L. (ed) (1993) *The New Shorter Oxford English Dictionary.* Volume 1, A-M. Clarendon Press, Oxford

Burch, V. (2008) *Living Well with Pain and Illness: The mindful way to free yourself from suffering.* Piatkus Books

Chodron, P. (2005) *No Time to Lose: A Timely Guide to the Way of the Bodhisattva.* Shambhala Publications, Inc, Boston & London

Conger, J.P. (1988) *Jung and Reich: The Body as Shadow.* North Atlantic Books

de Marchi, L. (1976) "Sexual Repression and Individual Pathology". In Boadella, D. (ed) *In the Wake of Reich.* Coventure Ltd, London

Fenichel, O. (1945) *The Psychoanalytical Theory of Neurosis.* New York, Norton

Friedman, M. (1996). *Type A Behavior: Its Diagnosis and Treatment (Prevention in Practice Library).* Plenum Press, New York

Gendlin, E. (2003) *Focusing: How to gain direct access to you Body's Knowledge.* 25th Anniversary edition (Third edition). Rider

Books

Gore, A. (2000) *Earth in the Balance: Ecology and the Human Spirit.* Houghton Mifflin, New York

Johnson, W. (2000) *Aligned, Relaxed, Resilient: The Physical Foundations of Mindfulness.* Shambhala Publications Inc

Kabat-Zinn, J. (2005) *Full Catastrophe Living: Using the Wisdom of Your Body and Mind to Face Stress, Pain and Illness.* Delta Trade Paperback re-issue, Random House Inc. Fifteenth edition

Kamalashila (1992) *Meditation: The Buddhist Way of Tranquillity and Insight.* Windhorse Publications

Klein, J. (2002) *Our Need for Others and Its Roots in Infancy.* Brunner-Routlege. Taylor & Francis Group. Reprint of first edition, 1987

Kornfield, J. (1994) *A Path with Heart: A Guide Through the Perils and Promises of Spiritual Life.* Rider Books

Kornfield, J. (2000) *After the Ecstasy, the Laundry: How the Heart Grows Wise on the Spiritual Path.* Rider Books. The Random House Group Ltd

Kurtz, R. (1985) *Hakomi Therapy Training Manual.* Self-published

Kurtz, R. (1990) *Body-Centred Psychotherapy: The Hakomi Method.* LifeRhythm, USA.

Govinda, Lama Anagarika (1990) *Creative Meditation and Multi-Dimensional Consciousness.* Quest Press, USA

Lowen, A. (1994) *Bioenergetics: The Revolutionary Therapy That Uses the Language of the Body to Heal the Problems of the Mind.* Arkana. New edition

Lowen, A. (2003) *The Language of the Body: Physical Dynamics of Character Structure.* First Bioenergetics Press Edition, Florida, USA. Originally published by Grune and Stratton (1958) as *Physical Dynamics of Character Structure*

Lowen, A. (2005) *The Betrayal of the Body: The Psychology of Fear and Terror.* First Bioenergetics Press Edition. Originally published by Macmillan Publishing Company (1967)

Macy, J. and Young Brown, M. (1998) *Coming Back to Life: Practices to Reconnect Our Lives, Our World.* New Society Publishers

Mindell, A. (1990) *Working on Yourself Alone: Inner Dreambody Work.* Penguin Arkana

Ratnadharini (2005) *Karma and the Consequences of Our Actions* (Online audio file: MP3). Free Buddhist Audio website. Talk number 4 of a series of 5 talks on The Four Mind-Turning Reflections, given by women at the Tiratanaloka Retreat Centre in Wales. This reference is taken from a conversation between Ratnadharini and Sangharakshita which is in chapter 2 of this talk. The chapter is entitled: "The 5 niyamas and the karma niyama; karma-vipaka – pleasurable and painful".
http://www.freebuddhistaudio.com/series/details?ser=X25 accessed 28/1/11

Ray, R.A. (2008) *Touching Enlightenment: Finding Realization in the Body.* Sounds True Inc. Boulder, Colorado

Reich, W. (1990) *Character Analysis.* Third edition. Farrar, Straus and Giroux (FSG), New York

Sangharakshita (1990) *Vision and Transformation: An Introduction to the Buddha's Noble Eightfold Path.* Windhorse Publications

Sangharakshita (1993) *The Drama of Cosmic Enlightenment: Parables, Myths, and Symbols of the White Lotus Sutra.* Windhorse Publications

Sangharakshita (1995) *Complete Poems 1941/1994.* Windhorse Publications

Sangharakshita (1998) *What is the Dharma? The Essential Teachings of the Buddha.* Windhorse Publications

Sangharakshita (1999) *The Bodhisattva Ideal.* Windhorse Publications

Sangharakshita (2002) *Creative Symbols of Tantric Buddhism.* Windhorse Publications

Sangharakshita (2003) *Living with Awareness: A Guide to the Satipatthana Sutta.* Windhorse Publications

Schützenberger, A.A. (1998*) The Ancestor Syndrome: Transgenerational Psychotherapy and the Hidden Links in the*

Family Tree. Routledge

Soothill, W.E. (1987) *The Lotus of the Wonderful Law or The Lotus Gospel.* Curzon Press Ltd in association with the Clarendon Press at the University of Oxford

Smith, E.W.L. (1985) *The Body in Psychotherapy.* McFarland and Company, Inc Publishers, USA

Staunton, T. (ed). (2002) *Body Psychotherapy (Advancing Theory in Therapy).* Routledge

Stromsted, T. (1998) "The Dance and the Body in Psychotherapy: Reflections and Clinical Examples". In Johnson, D. H. and Grand, I.J. (eds) *The Body in Psychotherapy: Inquiries in Somatic Psychology.* North Atlantic Books, Berkeley, California

Suzuki, S. (1993) *Zen Mind, Beginner's Mind.* Weatherhill Inc, New York. Eleventh reprint of first edition

Thich Nhat Hanh (1998) *The Heart of the Buddha's Teaching: Transforming Suffering into Peace, Joy and Liberation.* Rider Press

Totton, N. (2003) *Body Psychotherapy: An Introduction.* Open University Press

Totton, N. (2008) Email to Kamalamani, 25 September 2008

Totton, N. and Edmondson, E. (1988) *Reichian Growth Work: Melting the Blocks to Life and Love.* 1st edition. Nature and Health Books

Totton, N. and Edmondson, E. (2009) *Reichian Growth Work: Melting the Blocks to Life and Love.* Second edition. PCCS Books, Ross-on-Wye

Totton, N. and Jacobs, M. (2001) *Character and Personality Types.* Open University Press

Trungpa, Chogyam (1973) *Cutting Through Spiritual Materialism.* Shambhala Publications, Inc, Boston, Massachusetts

Tsogyal, Y. (2008) *The Life and Liberation of Padmasambhava (Part II).* Canto 103. Dharma Publishing, US

UNWCED (The United Nations World Commission on Environment and Development) (1987) *Our Common Future.* Oxford Paperbacks

Vessantara (1994) *Meeting the Buddhas: A Guide to Buddhas, Bodhisattvas, and Tantric Deities.* Windhorse Publications

Welwood, J. (2000) *Towards a Psychology of Awakening: Buddhism, Psychotherapy and the Path of Personal and Spiritual Transformation.* Shambhala Publications Inc, USA

Williams, M., Teasdale, J., Segal, Z., and Kabat-Zinn, J. (2007) *The Mindful Way Through Depression: Freeing Yourself from Chronic Unhappiness.* The Guilford Press Inc

Bibliography

Abram, D. (1997) *The Spell of the Sensuous: Perception and Language in a More-Than-Human World*. Vintage Books

Afford, P. (1994) "Focusing." In Jones, D. (ed) *Innovative Therapy: A Handbook*. Open University Press

Bernstein, J.S. (2005) *Living in the Borderland: The Evolution of Consciousness and the Challenge of Healing Trauma*. Routledge, London and New York

Brazier, C. (2003) *Buddhist Psychology: Liberate your mind, embrace life*. Robinson, London

Brazier, D. (2001) *The Feeling Buddha: An Buddhist Psychology of Character, Adversity and Passion*. Robinson, London

Caldwell, C. (1996) *Getting Our Bodies Back: Recovery, Healing and Transformation through Body-Centred Psychotherapy*. Shambhala Publications Inc

Conger, J.P. (1994) *The Body in Recovery: Somatic Psychotherapy and the Self*. Frog Ltd, North Atlantic Books, Berkeley, CA

Corrigal, J., Payne, H. and Wilkinson, H. (ed) (2006) *About a Body: Working with the Embodied Mind in Psychotherapy*. Routledge Books. London and New York

Cotter, S. (1996) "Using Bioenergetics to Develop Managers." *Journal of Management Development*. Volume 15, Issue 3, pages 8-16

Cranmer, D. (1994) "Core Energetics." In Jones, D. (ed) *Innovative Therapy: A Handbook*. Open University Press

Damasio, A. (2000) *The Feeling of What Happens: Body, Emotion and the Making of Consciousness*. Vintage Books, London

Ferruci, P. (1990) *What We May Be: Visions and Techniques of Psychosynthesis*. Aquarius

Freud, S. (1950) *The Ego and the Id*. London: Hogarth Press

Gerhardt, S. (2004) *Why Love Matters: How Affection Shapes a Baby's Brain*. Routledge

Gilbert, P. (2005) *Compassion: Conceptualisations, Research and Use in Psychotherapy*. Routledge

Harcourt, W. (2009) *Body Politics in Development: Critical Debates in Gender and Development*. Zed Books, London and New York

Heckler, R. (1983) "Entering into the Place of Conflict." In Welwood, J. (ed) *Awakening the Heart: East/West Approaches to Psychotherapy and the Healing Relationship*. Shambhala Publications Inc

Herman, J. (1997) *Trauma and Recovery: The Aftermath of Violence – from Domestic Abuse to Political Terror*. BasicBooks, A Member of the Perseus Books Group

Ingram, C. (2004) *Passionate Presence: Experiencing the Seven Qualities of Awakened Awareness*. Gotham Books, reprint edition

Johnson, D. Hanlon (ed) (1997) *Groundworks: Narratives of Embodiment*. North Atlantic Books, Berkeley, California

Keleman, S. (1975) *The Human Ground: Sexuality, Self and Survival*. Center Press, Berkeley, CA

Lakoff, G. and Johnson, M. (1999) *Philosophy in the Flesh: The Embodied Mind and Its Challenge to Western Thought*. BasicBooks, A Member of the Perseus Books Group

Laing, R.D. (1970) *The Divided Self*. Penguin Books Ltd

Levine, P. with Frederick, A. (1997) *Waking the Tiger: Healing Trauma*. North Atlantic Books, Berkeley, California

Levine, P. and Kline, M. (2007) *Trauma Through a Child's Eyes: Awakening the Ordinary Miracle of Healing*. North Atlantic Books

Macy, J. (1991) *Mutual Causality in Buddhism and General Systems Theory: The Dharma of Natural Systems*. State University of New York Press (SUNY)

Macnaughton, I. (ed) (2004) *Body, Breath and Consciousness: A Somatics Anthology*. North Atlantic Books, Berkeley, California

Maitland, J. (1995) *Spacious Body: Explorations in Somatic Ontology*. North Atlantic Books

Merleau-Ponty, M. (1962) *Phenomenology of Perception: An Introduction.* Routledge and Kegan Paul

Mindell, A. and Mindell, A. (1992) *Riding the Horse Backwards: Process Work in Theory and Practice.* Penguin Arkana

Mindell, A. (2001) *The Dreammaker's Apprentice: Using Heightened States of Consciousness to Interpret Dreams.* Hampton Roads Publishing Company Inc

Paramananda (2007) *The Body: The Art of Meditation series.* Windhorse Publications

Rahula, W. (1974) *What the Buddha Taught.* Grove Press, an imprint of Grove/Atlantic Inc, NY. Second Edition

Roszak, T. (1994) "Definition of Ecopsychology". *The Ecopsychology Newsletter,* No 1, Spring. Page 8

Rothschild, B. (2000) *The Body Remembers: The Psychophysiology of Trauma and Trauma Treatment.* W.W. Norton & Company, New York, London

Rowan, J. (1988) *Ordinary Ecstasy: Humanistic Psychology in Action.* Routledge, London and New York

Sangharakshita (1990) *A Guide to the Buddhist Path.* Windhorse Publications

Sangharakshita (1993) *A Survey of Buddhism: Its Doctrines and Methods Through the Ages.* Windhorse Publications. Reprinted seventh edition

Segal, Z.V., Williams, J.M.G., and Teasdale, J.D. (2002) *Mindfulness-Based Cognitive Therapy for Depression: A New Approach to Preventing Relapse.* Guilford Press

Stern, D. (1990) *Diary of a Baby: What Your Child Sees, Feels, and Experiences.* BasicBooks, A Member of the Perseus Books Group

Subhuti (2001) *The Buddhist Vision: A Path to Fulfilment.* Windhorse Publications. First Windhorse edition

Totton, N. (2002) "Foreign bodies: recovering the history of body psychotherapy". In Staunton, T. (ed) *Body Psychotherapy.* Routledge

Totton, N. (ed) (2005) *New Dimensions in Body Psychotherapy.* Open University Press

Totton N. (2007) "Ancestors", unpublished paper from the author

Welwood, J. (1983) "On Psychotherapy and Meditation". In Welwood, J. (ed) *Awakening the Heart: East/West Approaches to Psychotherapy and the Healing Relationship.* Shambhala Publications Inc

West, W. (1994) "Post-Reichian Therapy". In Jones, D. (ed) *Innovative Therapy: A Handbook.* Open University Press

Yalom, I. (2001) *The Gift of Therapy: Reflections on being a Therapist.* Piatkus Books

info@kamalamani.co.uk
www.kamalamani.co.uk

Index

BOOKS

O is a symbol of the world, of oneness and unity. In different cultures it also means the "eye," symbolizing knowledge and insight. We aim to publish books that are accessible, constructive and that challenge accepted opinion, both that of academia and the "moral majority."

Our books are available in all good English language bookstores worldwide. If you don't see the book on the shelves ask the bookstore to order it for you, quoting the ISBN number and title. Alternatively you can order online (all major online retail sites carry our titles) or contact the distributor in the relevant country, listed on the copyright page.

See our website www.o-books.net for a full list of over 500 titles, growing by 100 a year.

And tune in to myspiritradio.com for our book review radio show, hosted by June-Elleni Laine, where you can listen to the authors discussing their books.